THE NEW RIGHT:
WE'RE READY TO LEAD

THE NEW RIGHT: WE'RE READY TO LEAD

RICHARD A. VIGUERIE

The Viguerie Company

ISBN: 09604814-2-7
Library of Congress Catalog Card No.: 81-50472

Printed in the United States of America

Dedication

To my mother and father.

How can anyone ever   adequately thank his parents for   their   love,   sacrifice,   understanding,   guidance, direction, patience, their always helpful hand, all of which seems to flow without end?

From a grateful son—thank you.

Acknowledgements

I have been thinking about and collecting notes, articles and other material for this book for the past four years, I suddenly realized that the fall of 1980—when perhaps the most important presidential election in the 20th century will be held—was the time it should be published. I am indebted to many people for helping me publish this book on short notice.

I want to thank fellow conservatives Morton Blackwell, John Lofton, Howard Phillips, Jim Martin, Joe Sobran and Bill Rhatican for their suggestions and criticisms.

I have drawn heavily upon *Conservative Digest* and *The New Right Report* for many of the facts and figures which fill the book.

I wish to also acknowledge the help of John Coyne and Curt Smith. I am especially indebted for the editorial assistance of a very old friend, Lee Edwards, without whose help the first edition of this book would not have been possible.

Lastly, I wish to give special thanks to Ann Stone, Peter McCarty, Walt Longyear and David Bufkin for their invaluable assistance on the present edition.

Introduction by
Jerry Falwell

At this present hour, there can be no questioning the retrogression of America's stability as a free and healthy nation. In the last several years, Americans have literally stood by and watched as godless, spineless leaders have brought our nation floundering to the brink of death.

Too many of our top governmental officials, including judges in high places, legislators, bureaucrats, and politicians, have cared more about getting a vote than about courageously standing for what is right and good for America. Considering that the stability of any group, whether it be a family or a nation, rises and falls upon leadership, it is no wonder that we find America depraved, decadent, and demoralized today.

As a parent and as a God-fearing citizen, I respect Mr. Viguerie's courage to speak out regarding liberals and their actions that have significantly occasioned America's perilous condition. Mr. Viguerie speaks with candor. He is blunt and to the point. The vacuum of leadership in America must be filled. Conservative Americans must now take the helm and guide America back to a position of stability and greatness.

Granted that the writer is hardly wholly objective since he himself is one of the key figures in the New Right, nevertheless, I believe that the book provides insight into the thinking of men and women who are leading a movement which, if anything, has been underrated by the news media as to its ultimate impact in American politics.

Mr. Viguerie uses the term the "New Right" to speak of those moral citizens who now must come together and let their voice be heard, those as he puts it:

"hard-working citizens sick and tired of high taxes and ever-rising inflation;

small businessmen angry at excessive government regulations and federal red tape;

born-again Christians disturbed about sex on TV and in movies;

parents opposed to forced busing;

supporters of the right to life and against federal financing of abortions;

middle class Americans tired of Big Government, Big Business, Big Labor and Big Education telling us what to do and what not to do;

pro-defense citizens alarmed by appeasement and weakness in U.S. foreign policy."

Mr. Viguerie has not detailed a new group; he has described the backbone of our country—those citizens who are pro-family, pro-moral, pro-life, and pro-American, who have integrity and believe in hard work, those who pledge allegiance to the flag and proudly sing our national anthem. He has described that group of citizens who love their country and are willing to sacrifice for her. America was built on faith in God, on integrity, and on hard work. Mr. Viguerie clearly names and points out the actions of those who have not been committed to these principles and have thus led to the weakening and the humiliation of a once great America.

It is now time for moral Americans to band together in a collective voice and make the difference in America by exerting an effort to make their feelings known. The godless minority of treacherous individuals who have been permitted to formulate national policy must now realize they do not represent the majority. They must be made to see that moral Americans are a powerful group who will no longer permit them to destroy our country with their godless, liberal philosophies.

The movement made up of conservative Americans can no longer be ignored and silenced. America's destiny awaits its action. Your children's future welfare will be decided by your present involvement.

Table of Contents

I

Why the New Right Is Winning

The election of 1980 came as a great shock to Americans who depended on the establishment media for their forecasts.

Not only did Ronald Reagan win the Presidency in an electoral landslide of historic proportions. For the first time in nearly a generation, Republicans took over the Senate.

Nationally known liberal Democrats—George McGovern, Frank Church, John Culver, Warren Magnuson, Gaylord Nelson, Birch Bayh—went down to defeat. The nation's leading liberal Republican senator (one of the few remaining after the 1978 elections) went down too: Jacob Javits lost to Alfonse D'Amato.

Americans learned early on the evening of November 4 that the election the media had called a "cliffhanger" was going to be, instead, a rout.

It was not until the next morning, when they woke to find the Senate in Republican hands, that they began to sense the full dimensions of the conservative revolution.

Suddenly it was the most cautious forecasters who looked most foolish. It was the people who had played it "safe" who had proved wildly wrong.

A few of us were not surprised. We in the New Right had been working for this moment for many years. We saw that our labors were bearing fruit, and we said so.

In the first edition of this book, written in the summer of 1980 and published six weeks *before* the election, I wrote:

"I firmly believe that we are on the brink of capturing one of those Houses, the U.S. Senate, perhaps this year and almost surely by 1982."

At the time it must have sounded as if I hadn't been reading the papers!

On the night of November 4, history walked in on the liberals uninvited.

● Ronald Reagan, the country's foremost conservative politician since 1966, won the Presidency of the United States.

● His popular vote total topped that of the incumbent President, the highly-publicized third-party candidate John Anderson, and all the splinter-party standard-bearers *combined*.

● His electoral college margin—489 to 49—was among the greatest in history. And among challengers facing incumbents, only Franklin Roosevelt in 1932—with a three-year Depression on his side—did better.

Meanwhile, in the Senate races, the results were just as astonishing.

Backed by the support and organization of the New Right, conservatives like Steve Symms of Idaho, Don Nickles of Oklahoma, Bob Kasten of Wisconsin, Jeremiah Denton of Alabama, John East of North Carolina, Charles Grassley of Iowa, James Abdnor of South Dakota, Dan Quayle of Indiana, and the only woman to win, Paula Hawkins of Florida, stepped forth to offer the nation a new generation of conservative congressional leadership.

While we didn't win all our battles—liberals like Colorado's Gary Hart and California's Alan Cranston managed to retain office by talking like conservatives—the results were even better than we had expected. But we knew it was a definite possibility.

We knew it *might* happen—because we were *making* it happen.

It has been obvious for a long time that conservatism is rising and liberalism is declining. Despite all the talk in the media about "trends," "cliffhangers," and "last-minute shifts," the plain truth is that more and more Americans are sick of liberalism—and aren't afraid to say so.

The election of 1980 was the first modern conservative landslide. But it wasn't the first anti-liberal landslide.

In 1968 two anti-liberal candidates, Richard Nixon and George Wallace, won a combined 57 percent of the popular vote against the well-liked—but liberal—incumbent Vice President, Hubert Humphrey.

In 1972 Nixon, never very popular, won more than 60% of the total vote against the flamingly liberal George McGovern, who carried only one state (not even his home state of South Dakota).

Jimmy Carter didn't win election as a liberal. In the 1976 primaries he presented himself as the most conservative candidate in the field, and it was not until after he was safely in office that it became clear he intended to be a liberal President.

Even in 1980, when Democrats were sick of Carter, he won primaries—when his opponent was the even further left Edward Kennedy. Meanwhile, Ronald Reagan piled up victories against conservative, moderate and liberal candidates in his own party.

After the televised debate a week before the election, an ABC phone-in poll gave Reagan a 2 to 1 edge over Carter. Many others in media denounced the poll as "unscientific."

Maybe it was. But the election on November 4 wasn't conducted in a laboratory either. The ABC poll was just one more sign of the times—for anyone who was interested.

All the signs pointed one way. They've been pointing that way for years, and years, and years. They still do.

America is basically a conservative country. The potential for conservative revolt has always been there, under the most favorable conditions. But those conditions have to be made.

That's where the New Right comes in.

For many years, conservatives were frustrated. We had no way to translate our vision into reality.

3

Most importantly, we lacked a vehicle to carry our message to the voters without going through the filter of the liberal-leaning news media.

During the 1950s, 1960s, and most of the 1970s liberal politicians were able to make speeches that sounded as if they were written by Barry Goldwater. The liberals could come home on weekends and make speeches calling for a strong America, attacking waste in Washington, and complaining about big government. Then, on Monday, they could go back to Washington and vote to block new weapons systems, to give away the Panama Canal, to increase taxes, to create new government agencies, and to weaken the CIA and FBI.

Occasionally, liberal politicians would visit Communist leaders like Fidel Castro and return to the U.S. with wonderful words of praise for the Cuban dictator, praise that most voters in South Dakota or Idaho never heard.

Why did the voters in South Dakota, Idaho, Iowa, Indiana, and Wisconsin not know about their congressmen's and senators' double lives—conservative-sounding at home, actively liberal in Washington or abroad?

Because most of the national (and some of the local) media didn't report the double life the politicians were leading.

Thanks to the New Right, the "people's right to know"—which the establishment media pay loud lipservice to, when it serves their own purposes—finally became a reality.

"You can't turn back the clock."

How often we hear this line from liberals. What they really mean is that we shouldn't try to correct their mistakes.

Well, the New Right has news for them. We aren't in the business of turning back clocks.

It's the Left that has tried to stop the clock and even bring back evils civilization has left behind.

• It's the Left that has re-introduced guild privileges based on compulsory unionism, government-imposed racial and sexual discrimination, and oppressive taxes.

• It's the Left that favors a society based on state regulation, supervision, and coercion.

- It's the Left that has defended and even promoted pornography and abortion. (The clock has stopped forever for eight million unborn American children.)
- It's the Left that focuses its compassion on the criminal rather than his victims.
- It's the Left that attacks our allies rather than our enemies.
- It's the Left that favors the non-producers over the people who work.
- It's the Left that encourages American women to feel that they are failures if they want to be wives and mothers.
- It's the Left that tears apart families and neighbors by the forced busing of children.
- It's the Left that has failed to protest Communist slavery and religious persecution—evils afflicting 1.8 *billion* human beings.
- It's the Left that's fought to keep prayer out of the schools.
- It's the Left that allowed ruthless Communist takeovers in Vietnam, Laos, Cambodia and Afghanistan.
- It's the Left that allowed the takeover of Iran, one of America's strongest allies, by a group of terrorists and extremists.
- It's the Left who crippled the CIA and FBI.
- It's the Left who sold the Russian computers and other sophisticated equipment used to oppress their people.

Liberalism has pitted itself against the best instincts of the American people. Journalist Tom Bethell says the abortion issue alone has destroyed the liberals' "moral monopoly."

Put simply, most Americans no longer look up to liberals. They look down on them.

Liberals have long sensed this. They have tried to make their mistakes irreversible and election-proof. As far as possible, they have sought to turn the powers of government over to the courts and administrative agencies— that is, to unelected and unaccountable public officials.

They have found other ways to impose their will. One of the most sophisticated has been deficit spending—producing an inflation that reduces blue-collar workers' real pay by pushing them into what used to be executive tax brackets. By such means liberals have increased government's grip on our wealth without openly raising tax rates.

Somebody had to call a halt to this devious elitism. What used to be liberalism has turned into socialism on the installment plan.

With the New Right, America has found a new voice. In 1980, that voice rang out—loud and clear.

The voters of Idaho and South Dakota finally got to know the *real* Frank Church and the *real* George McGovern—the ones Fidel Castro knows.

Because conservatives have mastered the new technology, we've been able to bypass the Left's near-monopoly of the national news media.

The New Right has also had its own ready-made network: the thousands of conservative Christian ministers whose daily broadcasts on local and national radio and TV reach an audience of 27 million. Every week, approximately 20 million people view just three such ministers—Jerry Falwell, Pat Robertson, and James Robison.

Until now this whole culture has been a dark continent to the Northeast, coastal-based national media. But these ministers are attacking issues the national media hardly mention: issues like worldwide Communist aggression, school prayer, sex on TV, the failures of the public schools. The conservative ministers are in touch with the people, and now they are in touch with each other.

The conservatism was always there. It took the New Right to give it leadership, organization, and direction.

The key word is *leadership*. Conservatives have had no lack of brilliant thinkers, brilliant writers, brilliant debaters, brilliant spokesmen. But none of these is the same thing as a leader.

George Gallup has found that 49% of registered voters in the U.S. now place themselves "right of center"—as against only 29% who say they are "left of center" and only 10% who call themselves "middle of the road."

And yet, with this tremendous potential support, the Republican Party has proved itself incapable of even mounting a consistent and effective opposition, much less rallying that 49% behind an agenda of its own. If it can't find its base with both hands, how is it going to lead the whole nation?

The New Right has proved it can lead. We're doing it. Leadership doesn't just show up on the first Tuesday in November. It has to be out there ahead of time—organizing, mailing, phoning, advertising, informing, getting names on the ballot.

It's fine for the analysts and pundits to talk about "trends." But "trends" don't win elections. People do.

It sounds plausible to explain the pollsters' failure to predict the 1980 results by referring to a hypothetical "last-minute shift" to Reagan and the Republicans. But it would be an amazing coincidence for so many million people to abruptly shift at the same instant. This explanation overlooks the demonstrated conservatism of the American people and the results of active conservative organization in this campaign.

There are no impersonal "trends." There was no national last-minute "shift." The people didn't suddenly fall in love with the Republican Establishment. These are fig-leaf excuses of the establishment media who were so far out of touch with the country that they missed all the signals the voters were sending.

The simple truth is that there is a new majority in America—and it's being led by the New Right.

II

The New Right:
Myth, Menace, or Mainstream?

The New Right is the most important force to appear on the American scene in decades. That's not intended as a boast. I think it's a matter of simple fact.

Strategically, our most vital component in 1980 may have been Terry Dolan's National Conservative Political Action Committee. It was NCPAC that targeted six liberal senators for defeat—and saw four of them fall.

But numerically and perhaps historically, our most important asset is Dr. Jerry Falwell's Moral Majority. The Moral Majority showed the enormous power religious people can have for good in America—if only they rouse themselves and don't leave the field to the Reverend Jesse Jackson, the Reverend William Sloane Coffin, Father Robert Drinan, and the National Council of Churches.

The role of Reverend Jerry Falwell's Moral Majority and their work to register several million new conservative Christian voters is well known.

In 1980 alone, the Moral Majority helped 2.5 million voters register for the first time. Thanks to it and similar groups, the nation's evangelical Christians, who had favored Jimmy Carter over Gerald Ford by 56% to 43% in 1976, went for Reagan over Carter by 56% to 34% in 1980!

Less well known is the major role played by people like Ed McAteer who in 1979 organized the Religious Round Table. From July 1980 to October of 1980, Ed organized public affairs briefings in towns and cities from Florida to California attended by approximately 40,000 conservative religious leaders including over 20,000 preachers.

After attending one to three days of speeches by Jerry Falwell, James Robison, Paul Weyrich, Howard Phillips, Phyllis Schlafly and many other national conservative leaders, most of these preachers would go back to the several hundred members of their churches and explain to them the danger America faced from liberals and humanists.

At one of these 3-day public affairs briefings in Dallas, Texas, Reagan spoke to 18,000 religious leaders.

Throughout the summer and fall of 1980 the word went out through these religious Paul Reveres (Jerry Falwell, Ed McAteer, Bob Billings, Adrian Rogers, Charles Stanley, Jim Kennedy, James Robison and many others) that America was in danger and only Ronald Reagan could cure her.

Both NCPAC and the Moral Majority encountered violent opposition. This was only natural. Any establishment will feel there is something subversive about organizations that manage to succeed outside the establishment-approved channels.

The establishment media have spoken freely of New Right "hit lists," making it sound more as if we had sent assassination teams into Iowa rather than simply taken an active role in the democratic process.

Throughout the campaign, these media reported our activities with alarm. Though they didn't expect such sweeping victories for New Right-backed candidates, they sensed that we posed a definite menace to at least some of the liberal favorites.

They were right. Their worst fears were surpassed by the results.

Before and after the election, there have been strenuous efforts to belittle our contribution. Liberals, "moderate" Republicans, and even some Washington-based conservative pundits began to insist we hadn't really had much to do with the outcome of the election.

For one thing, The Congressional Club, The Fund For A Conservative Majority, and NCPAC raised and spent over $8,000,000 to help elect Reagan completely independent of the official Reagan presidential campaign.

Liberals who had been right about us before the election, were now trying to convince the public we were a harmless lot after all.

They all agreed—after the fact—that the elections they had failed to predict merely bore witness to an impersonal conservative "trend" which was bound to happen. Suddenly they were talking as if the events they had been unable to foresee had been so foreordained that no human action could have affected them one way or the other. They didn't explain why, if it had been inevitable, they couldn't see it coming.

If they prefer to think it was a one-shot accident, that the New Right had nothing to do with it, well, frankly, *good.* Just keep thinking that, gentlemen. Please don't change your minds about us. Leave your defenses in place right where they are. We won't change anything either. We'll just do the same thing in 1982, and you can say it was another, fluke, inevitable trend, or whatever you want to call it!

But our opponents had better have a convention to get their attacks coordinated. If some of them think we're completely harmless, others are downright hysterical.

Rabbi Alexander M. Schindler, president of the United Hebrew Congregation and an outspoken liberal activist, has called on American Jews to form "coalitions of decency against the chilling power of the radical right." He blames the Moral Majority for what he calls "the most serious outbreak of anti-Semitism in America since the end of World War II."

Rabbi Schindler admits that Dr. Falwell is not personally anti-Semitic—as well he might, since Menachem Begin in 1980 publicly honored Dr. Falwell for his staunch support of Israel. But he still holds him somehow responsible for those who are anti-Semitic, without explaining clearly how this can be, who the actual anti-Semites are, or where the evidence of the "outbreak" may be.

The American Civil Liberties Union accuses the Moral Majority and other New Right groups of trying to destroy the Bill of Rights and impose "a nightmare of political and religious orthodoxy." But the ACLU, like Rabbi Schindler, fails to provide a shred of evidence.

These are serious charges. If they are false, they are libelous. And in the absence of proof, it's only fair to presume they are false. When Joe McCarthy charged there were Communists in the State Department, he was required to name names and offer documentation. To this day the liberals use McCarthy's name as a byword for smear tactics.

And yet, sadly enough, when the liberals themselves use such tactics, the media often carry their smears without question and, in some cases, without even asking the victims of these baseless charges to reply. The media seem content to serve as passive vehicles for liberals' wildest accusations.

By so doing, the media in effect automatically take the side of the accuser against the accused.

Is this what George McGovern means when he talks of setting up a "coalition of common sense"? Or is it more like what liberals call "McCarthyism"?

What about due process? What about the presumption of innocence? Isn't the burden of proof supposed to be on the accuser, according to the American tradition of fair play? Where are the investigative journalists who, if they are open-minded about the issue, should be getting to the bottom of the case?

All too probably, the media themselves have been taken in by the myth that liberals stand for the rights of the accused. Only conservatives are thought to engage in character assassination.

Conservatives know better. In 1964, following Barry Goldwater's nomination as the Republican presidential candidate, California's Governor Edmund "Pat" Brown, a liberal Democrat, said: "I smell the stench of Nazism. I hear the march of storm troopers." George Meany added that there was "a parallel between Senator Barry Goldwater and Adolf Hitler." (These remarks were made all the more offensive by the fact that Goldwater's grandfather had been a Jewish immigrant from Poland.)

No amount of vitriol from liberal mouths seems to change the myth of innate liberal nobility.

But it was Jane Fonda, not Phyllis Schlafly, who called America "a war machine" and "a murderer."

It was Bella Abzug, not Representative Marjorie Holt (R—Maryland), who branded America "imperialistic. . . power mad. . . a vehicle for murder and oppression."

It was Andrew Young, not William F. Buckley, Jr., who termed our ally Great Britain "a police state."

During the 1972 campaign, George McGovern called America's policies in Vietnam "the most barbaric and inhumane since Adolf Hitler."

His running-mate, Sargent Shriver, called President Nixon "the greatest murderer in the world today."

And during the 1980 campaign Jimmy Carter, Andrew Young, Patricia Roberts Harris, and other Carter cronies did their best to tar Ronald Reagan as a racist and war-monger.

This time, happily, it backfired. Carter's desperate viciousness helped finish him off politically, and many in the national media deserve full credit for seeing to it that Reagan got a fair shake.

As the New Right has developed its own communications network, the older media have begun to come to terms with us. We are now receiving far more fair and even favorable coverage than we would have counted on.

Some liberals, like Senator Tsongas of Massachusetts, are starting to face the fact: liberalism has failed. Others, like Senator Patrick Moynihan of New York and CBS radio commentator Roger Wilkins, acknowledge that the fresh thinking in American politics these days is coming almost exclusively from the conservative side.

But I'll let you in on a little secret. Except for supply-side economics—a theory that has been brilliantly developed and put to work by Congressman Jack Kemp of New York—there aren't that many new conservative ideas. Most of the ideas have been around for a long time.

What is really new is that conservatives have learned how to recruit, how to organize and how to successfully market ideas. For the first time, the American people are hearing the conservative's solutions to problems.

Many liberals, who are accustomed to doing all the talking, haven't quite got used to listening yet. As Bill Buckley once put it, "Though liberals do a great deal of talking about hearing other points of view, it sometimes shocks them to learn that there *are* other points of view."

Usually they can't quite bring themselves to admit that it's perfectly legitimate for conservatives to do what liberals have always done. Conservatives have patiently endured years and years of hearing political sermons from radical chic clergymen who give the appearance of being more interested in saving whales than souls.

But when clergymen on *our* side speak out, it becomes a "menace," a "threat" to the separation of church and state. Why is it a violation of the Constitution when Cardinal Madeiros of Boston sends a letter to his churches reminding Catholic voters that it's wrong to abet abortion through politics, but not wrong when Jesse Jackson stands in the pulpit to directly endorse Jimmy Carter?

Beyond all the feeble excuses and double standards they raise, liberals probably just have a gut feeling that it just isn't right for us to do what they feel they have an exclusive right to do. Deep down, the establishment feels that the New Right is just plain uppity.

In a way, they remind me of the old segregationists who used to insist (sincerely) that they liked blacks—but not these young aggressive blacks. The ones they liked, of course, were the ones who didn't pose a threat to their status quo. Some of the Uncle Toms didn't like them either: they had found their own privileged niche within the status quo; blacks pressing for change were a threat. I sometimes think there are Republican "Uncle Toms" who were doing just fine until the New Right came along.

Liberals will tell you that some of their best friends are conservatives—"responsible" conservatives that is. They mean it. And they are perfectly right.

As Professor Charles Moser of George Washington University has put it: "The liberals have developed their own definition of a 'responsible conservative,' by which they happily measure New Rightists in order to pronounce them 'irresponsible.' In the liberal vocabulary, a 'conservative' is merely a 'fiscal conservative,' that is, one who has no objection in principle to new government programs which the liberals wish to introduce but simply wants to spend less money on them.

"The liberals find it easy to reach compromises with such conservatives by accepting a little less initially for their pet projects, secure in the knowledge that once such programs are established increased funding for them will be forthcoming. New Right conservatives, by contrast, oppose many government programs on principle, not merely on grounds of cost, arguing that there are certain areas in which government should not interfere regardless of finances."

So that what liberals mean when they say they like responsible conservatives but not these New Right type conservatives is they like ineffective "conservatives" like Jerry Ford but these effective New Right conservatives like Terry Dolan make them nervous.

I can certainly understand the liberals' fear of Terry Dolan, Paul Weyrich, Jerry Falwell, Ed McAteer, Morton Blackwell because they have proven themselves to be effective in defeating liberal candidates, liberal legislation, and building a conservative network of organizations that may soon replace the long-time dominant liberal organizations in power and effectiveness.

Irresponsible? We're so irresponsible we don't even mind losing a fight. We fight anyway. Where the "responsible" Republican tries to appease and compromise, we try to win. Or if we lose, we want to come out of the fight with an issue to use against the liberals in the next election.

Strange things happen when you fight. When you battle for a principle, you may lose the battle—but not the principle. The principle lives on, to shame and embarrass the winners. It stays in the public mind and may wind up on the agenda. Congressman Kemp has done this brilliantly, against the stern advice of more "responsible" members of his own party, with his persistent advocacy of the Kemp-Roth tax cut program.

Today, as a result, there's another Kemp-Roth advocate in town—in the Oval Office.

If we chose to be Uncle Toms, we too could be called "responsible" and "respectable." This is the liberals' reward to Republicans who compromise on essentials— who allow the liberal program to pass for a "bipartisan" program, as long as the initial spending outlays don't look too outrageous. But we refuse to make compromises that are really surrenders.

What liberals absolutely *don't* want, in the words of neoconservative Irving Kristol, is "a conservatism with strong ideas of its own about economic policy, social policy, or foreign policy—especially if these can pass academic muster and survive intellectual debate. Such a conservatism might actually affect public policy, even become a shaping force in American politics, and this is

14

simply impermissible. The very possibility of such a conservatism is a specter that haunts the liberal imagination and can propel it into frenzies of exorcism."

Sometimes the "unbeatable foe" turns out to be surprisingly beatable. Everyone in his (or her) right mind knew Phyllis Schlafly had to be crazy to try to stop the Equal Rights Amendment. Both parties had endorsed it. Both Houses of Congress had passed it overwhelmingly. It was sweeping like wildfire through the state legislatures. The big media were all for it.

And guess what? Today ERA is dead. It just goes to show: when you take on Phyllis Schlafly, you'd better have something more than just three U.S. Presidents, two Houses of Congress, two major parties, a bunch of legislatures, big labor, and the national media going for you!

The New Right has also helped defeat a few other "unbeatable" foes:

• We stopped the common situs picketing bill (primary credit for this must go to the heroic work of the National Right to Work Committee).

• We helped block ratification of SALT II.

• We helped defeat instant voter registration.

• We prevented the financing of congressional elections with taxpayers' money.

How much you can win even when you lose is best illustrated by our biggest battle of all: the Panama Canal treaties.

I'll say more about this key campaign later. Suffice it for now that our "responsible" brethren backed the treaties. Both parties supported them, even though the polls showed that the people intensely and overwhelmingly opposed—as many as 75% saying No!

The New Right decided to make a fight of it. We lost. There was just too much catching up to do. But we made an issue of it that carried over into the 1978 and 1980 senatorial races and will carry over into 1982.

Of course Panama is still a touchstone issue—one of those great questions that have a way of telling you who is, and who isn't, in harmony with the deepest sentiments of the American people.

The liberals aren't. The "responsible" Republicans aren't.

The New Right is.

That's why we're a "menace." Not a menace to the country. A menace to the status quo.

Because that status quo has been more than a menace to the country. It's been a disaster.

III

Why Liberalism Is Dying

It's very simple.

The Left is old and tired. The New Right is young and vigorous.

Most of the liberals' leaders of the past 30 years are gone—Adlai Stevenson, Walter Reuther, George Meany, Martin Luther King, Jr., Nelson Rockefeller, Hubert Humphery, Robert Kennedy.

And in 1978 and 1980, what remained of liberal political leadership took a terrible mauling at the polls. It's getting harder and harder to find an *elected* liberal in Washington!

Of course liberalism survives as an entrenched power. There is no shortage of *unelected* liberals. These are the only ones who can still afford the luxury of dismissing conservatism and the New Right.

Liberalism isn't just losing at the polls. It's losing in the battle of ideas. Conservatives and libertarians are winning Nobel Prizes and scoring victories in the universities as well. Some of the most brilliant conservative minds in the country are now teaching at Harvard.

Why is liberalism losing? That's simple too: because it is a "can't-do" philosophy.

It says America is past her peak. It calls for retreat abroad and no-growth economics at home. It attacks the productive forces of American society. It treats the American people as children who must be supervised and controlled and as defendants who must be presumed "racist" and "sexist" until proven otherwise.

Liberalism says No. No to freedom, No to growth, No to the future. Worst of all, it says No to American greatness. Liberals have taken a posture of denial and recrimination toward the American people. Instead of respecting their countrymen and trying to persuade them, liberals accuse, harass, blame, tax, regiment, and compel their fellow citizens.

Is it any wonder liberals lose elections? Is it any wonder liberals prefer to do business with the American public through the courts and bureaucracies, rather than through accountable, elected representatives?

To liberals, civil rights has come to mean not equality of opportunity but reverse racism and forced busing. Women's rights has come to mean denial of the first right of all human beings, regardless of sex: the right to life. Civil liberties has come to mean not the free exercise of religion but forbidding school children a daily moment of voluntary prayer. Compassion for the poor has come to mean contempt for the middle class.

One of the biggest lies of 20th century American politics is that liberals care about people and conservatives don't.

This is a bum rap put on us by liberals.

I suggest that it's conservatives who, by their actions, show real love and compassion for their fellow men.

And it's the liberals who seem to be able to close their eyes and turn their backs on the most massive outpouring of murder, slavery and crime ever known to man.

We should pray and work to help liberals understand how (1) their policies are responsible for turning Cambodia, Laos, Vietnam, parts of Africa and all of Eastern Europe over to the Communist slavemasters; (2) their policies of obsession with the rights of hardened criminals, drug pushers, the Mafia, and terrorists are primarily responsible for 141 violent crimes committed per hour in America.

If the liberals have such great love for their fellow man, what are their plans to help the 1.8 billion wretched souls held in slavery by the Communists, the tens of millions in America who are slaves to drugs and to welfare? Where are the liberals marching and demonstrating that something be done to stop one million violent crimes committed every year mostly against the minorities and senior citizens.

Those of us who are conservatives should hold our heads high and be proud of our record to help our fellow man.

Maybe success has spoiled liberalism. Whatever the cause, at some point in the last few years it crossed a threshold and turned into socialism.

Sociaiism is always idealistic in theory and brutal in actual practice. It talks about compassion, but resorts to coercion. In seeking to build utopias, it has to destroy the customs and freedoms of real people.

In the long run, all forms of socialism depend on force. We have seen liberalism degenerate into what the great French libertarian Frederic Bastiat called "organized plunder," taxing some for the benefit of others. And then they wonder what's wrong with "the economy"—when they themselves have punished production and made work unprofitable!

They pretend to hate only giant corporations. But in reality they inflict burdens and suffering on every laboring man and woman in America.

As Richard Weaver said, "Ideas have consequences." Liberalism's ideas are essentially negative. And so are its consequences.

At one time it may not have seemed that way. Jeffrey Hart has said it well:

"Only yesterday, it seems, liberalism was buoyant, open, confident. We had nothing to fear but fear itself. Liberalism spoke of economic expansion, of technology and science, of progress and of American power in the world. We would have 50 million jobs. We were the arsenal of democracy.

"But today liberalism is making the great refusal. It seems to see life, in Robert Frost's phrase, as a diminished thing. It is defensive and shrunken and it has opted out of the American tradition. . .

"The profound negativism of today's liberal defines the conservative opportunity. The conservative should be the voice of possibility and optimism, should embrace the future."

Amen. You have to wonder if Franklin Roosevelt himself would recognize today's shivering, stay-at-home liberals as his descendants. Frankly, I doubt it.

Often liberal intentions are good. They want to eliminate poverty. But then they make war on the best anti-poverty program the world has ever seen: the free market.

George Gilder, one of the finest young minds to identify himself with the New Right, has made an eloquent statement about why the free market is desirable not only materially but morally as well. "Poverty," he says, "is a matter not of income but of prospects."

Answering the charge that capitalism is based on greed, he goes on:

"The fact is, however, that capitalism thrives on religious faith and decays without it. Capitalist progress is based on the acceptance of risks that cannot be demonstrated to pay off in any one lifetime.

"Thus, it relies on faith in the future and in Providence.

"Capitalism depends not on greed but on giving, investment without a contracted return. The workers under capitalism are motivated not by crude economic rewards but by love of family. The entrepreneurs succeed to the extent that they are sensitive to the needs of others, and to the extent that others succeed. Altruism is the essence of the positive-sum game of capitalism."

Walter Lippmann observed that our system gave men "a way of producing wealth in which the good fortune of others multiplied their own."

But today's liberalism has adopted a socialistic philosophy that attacks the very foundations of production and closes off the future. It puts all its faith in government, which can't produce wealth, but can only take from those who do—and then turns on the producers and blames them for the resulting poverty!

You know, I have to smile when I read or hear that it is we conservatives who want to take America back to the 19th or 18th century.

I ask you: What could be more reactionary than Ralph Nader's proposal that the federal government issue charters for all U.S. corporations? It's downright medieval to say that the right of a business to function should come from government. Government can't create rights. It can only recognize them and protect them. This is the philosophy set forth in the Declaration of Independence: our inalienable rights come from God.

Once you admit that government can create rights, you have to grant government the power to deny them as well. This is exactly what has happened to the inalienable right to life in the case of abortion.

Liberals' misguided notions of "rights" often wind up hurting their intended beneficiaries. They say a 17-year-old with the equivalent of a fifth-grade education has the "right" to a minimum wage of $3.35 an hour. The most frequent result: the young man or woman becomes another statistic on the unemployment rolls.

I'm constantly amazed by liberals who say they are "for" more jobs and more income for ordinary people, but who have only contempt and even hatred for businesses, large and small, and particularly for profitable businesses.

How can you be for eggs but against chickens? Or for milk but against cows? Where do they think jobs come from?

During the decade of the 1980s the liberals will be at a major disadvantage against the conservatives.

If the New Right conservatives continue their tremendous momentum while the liberals continue debating the rejected socialist ideas of the 60s and 70s, then conservatives should significantly increase their victories and completely dominate the American political scene through the 20th century and into the 21st.

There are many reasons why I'm so optimistic but let me give you six of the major ones:

(1) First, the Left is about 8-10 years behind conservatives in the use of most of the new political technology. What is the new technology? It's using computers, direct mail, telephone marketing, TV (including cable TV) and radio, cassette tapes and toll-free numbers among other things to ask for contributions and for votes. Conservatives have identified about 4,000,000 contributors. I estimate that the liberals have identified less than 1,500,000.

And through the methods I describe in this book the conservatives have a good chance to increase their contributor base to 9,000,000 by January, 1984. But I doubt the number of contributors to liberal causes will exceed 2,500,000 by January, 1984.

About 85% of the approximately 50 direct mail experts who raise money for political causes are conservatives.

No college or university that I'm aware of offers a four year degree in direct response advertising.

Most everyone gets into direct mail accidentally and I estimate, if you have good training, it takes a minimum of five years before you can begin to think of yourself as a political direct mail expert.

It will probably take the Left the better part of eight years just to develop the trained personnel to handle their direct response marketing.

Reverend Jerry Falwell and his staff have over 20 years experience. James Robison has over 10 years. I have almost 20 years of national direct mail experience. Steve Winchell, whose direct mail advertising agency brilliantly handles most of the fund raising for the various national Republican committees, has been in political direct mail for 14 years. Steve was my executive vice president for most of the nine years he was with me. He formed Winchell and Associates in 1976.

Not all liberals are unaware of how far behind us the Left has fallen. Vic Kamber, 36, who heads a public relations firm servicing liberal/labor clients has for many years been trying to warn his liberal friends that conservatives were intelligently putting together the technology, the organizations and the money to defeat the Left.

Roger Craver, 39, who handled the John Anderson direct mail effort in 1980 and Richard Parker, 34, who is president of his own direct mail organization in California are two of the most talented liberal direct mail response experts.

These young liberals will be working hard to help the Left catch up to us conservatives. I personally feel that the future success of American liberals rests a great deal more with a few people such as Kamber, Craver, and Parker than with some of the better known liberal senators and governors.

If the Left doesn't quickly develop the ability to compete with us in direct mail and paid TV, and then use that expertise to build large effective organizations, we conservatives will have a much easier time of it.

(2) A substantial part of the finances for liberal organizations in the 1970s came from the federal government (*you the taxpayer*).

We can expect the Reagan Administration, primarily through the office of David Stockman, to quickly reduce that figure close to zero.

Millions of dollars the federal government gave in the 1970s to liberal organizations went to Caesar Chavez' United Farm Workers, Tom Hayden's and Jane Fonda's Western Sun, Planned Parenthood, Americans for Democratic Action, National Urban League, the Gay Community Center, Southern Christian Leadership Foundation, National Welfare Rights Organization and many, many others.

(3) In the 1976 elections about 70% of big business' political action committee (PAC) donations went to liberals. But that has already started changing.

In 1980 big business probably split the donations about even between conservatives and liberals.

But now with Reagan in the White House and conservative Republican senators like Orrin Hatch, Strom Thurmond, Jake Garn and Jesse Helms heading up most of the major senate committees, the liberals will be lucky to get 25% of the big business political action committee donations in 1982 and 1984.

Also corporations and foundations run by big businessmen have given large sums of money to liberal organizations—this should also significantly decrease.

(4) The liberals face another major problem in trying to get the money to finance their efforts.

It's well known that the vast majority of the supporters of liberal causes are under 40, or else they are on the lower end of the economic scale, and make less than $15,000 a year. Therefore, those most likely to contribute to liberal causes have very little money available to contribute.

Young voters are worried about having enough money for a car, mortgage, and tuition payments along with buying shoes and clothes for fast growing children.

So that when the voters have reached a time in life (50 years or older) when their children have left home and they are into the best money making period of their life, they are now voting conservative and they have money available to contribute to political causes.

(5) It's ironic that the liberal Democrats who are so fond of thinking of themselves as speaking for and representing the average citizen, receive most of the money for their candidates and organizations from big government, big business, big foundations and big labor.

And in the 1980s liberal interests will probably have to rely even more heavily on the forced dues of union members who are becoming more conservative every day. As they continue to press their members to pay for political causes they don't believe in, the rank-and-file will move further into our corner.

If the efforts in the courts and in Congress of the National Right to Work Committee and the National Right to Work Foundation — whose contributors give a total of over $5,000,000 per year, are successful in keeping the union officials from using the compulsory dues of their members for politics, the liberals will be at an enormous financial disadvantage.

(6) And if all of this is not enough, the liberals today simply do not have the issues that will cause millions of Americans who have not previously made a political contribution to send money.

I would not like to try and raise money for most of the liberal causes—(a) reducing the military budget; (b) promoting detente, including giving loans and credits to Communist countries; (c) giving the Panama Canal away; (d) no tax reductions; (e) no reduction of the federal budget; (f) expanding the welfare system; (g) continuing forced busing of children; (h) quotas; (i) affirmative action; (j) expanding the size of government and increasing its involvement in the life of Americans.

Sometime around the mid 60s the liberals, riding high on a false sense of security, began to rest on their momentum and success.

It's certainly easy to understand how a political movement that had achieved successes the Left had for the past 50 years would not feel the need to continue to explore the latest in technology, new ways of advertising and new ways of organizing.

To win elections you have to be able to market your candidates, causes, and issues to the American public.

And in order to raise money from the public in the 1980s you must have a knowledge of computers, direct mail and TV as it relates to fund raising, plus you have to have popular issues.

The Left has little of any of these. And when their money from the government and corporations is greatly reduced, the Left will experience a serious financial problem in the 1980s.

Yes, it's really very simple. Liberalism is almost stone cold dead in American politics. And conservatism is ready, willing, and able to take its place—because the New Right has made a profound difference in conservative effectiveness and capacity these last few years. That difference has been made possible by the emergence of dynamic, brilliant, determined young leaders in and out of Congress.

For example:

• The Heritage Foundation, headed by Ed Feulner, has given tough-minded conservatives in Congress an intellectual base for their battles.

• The Conservative Caucus, led by Howard Phillips, has provided leadership to mobilize grassroots sentiment and action.

• The Committee for the Survival of a Free Congress, directed by Paul Weyrich, and

• The National Conservative Political Action Committee, headed by Terry Dolan, have offered technical expertise, training, and money to right-of-center candidates of both parties.

• The Republican Study Committee—directed by Richard Dingman—and

• The Senate Steering Committee—directed by Margo Carlisle—are made up of conservative congressmen and senators who during the second half of the 1970s successfully united to stop left-wing legislation, to win congressional rules fights, to protect legislative minority rights, and to contest nominations to regulatory and other agencies—just to name a few of their battles.

• The National Right to Work Committee is a heroic example of a long-established group whose persistence has paid off. A few years ago many thought Right to Work was a lost cause. But since 1971 its supporter list has grown from a modest 25,000 to more than 1,000,000.

- The American Conservative Union is another older organization that's operated full tilt in lobbying efforts, coast-to-coast TV programs, and upbeat publications.
- Political action committees (PACs) like the Conservative Victory Fund have hired full-time staffs rather than using volunteers as in the past.

These groups have been joined by many others—Gun Owners of America, right-to-life groups, pro-family and religious groups. I'll mention more of them later.

As you can see, conservatives are now showing up to play political ball on time, fully equipped, in the correct ball park—and with a game plan for victory.

Meanwhile conservative leaders—not just spokesmen—have emerged in Congress. In the Senate, men like Orrin Hatch, Paul Laxalt, Jesse Helms, James McClure, Gordon Humphrey, Bill Armstrong. In the House, men like Phillip Crane, Mickey Edwards, Robert Dornan, Larry McDonald, Henry Hyde, Newt Gingrich, Jerry Solomon, Jim Jeffries, George Hansen.

As of 1981, they are joined by a host of others whose potential for leadership can't be predicted, though it is undoubtedly enormous. And there will be still others.

We are the people who reject the liberal line that America has had her day in the sun. We believe that America is still the land of opportunity, of optimism, of progress. We know that while the truths that made America great may have suffered an eclipse, they still blaze as brightly as ever.

We believe in God and the importance of the traditional family. We believe that the way to peace is to be stronger than any country that wants to conquer us. We believe in fiscal prudence, and in helping those—but only those—who truly cannot help themselves.

We are Christian and Jewish. We are Republican, Democratic, and independent. Our first commitment is to political principles, not to political parties.

We are mostly middle and working class. We wear a blue as well as a white collar.

We care about the social and cultural index of this nation as well as the Consumer Price Index.

We live and work mostly on Main Street, not Wall Street. We're more at home on the front porch than in the boardroom.

We are aggressive, committed, confident.

We don't give a darn about yesterday's defeats. We're interested in tomorrow's victories.

IV

From Houston to New York to Washington

I'm frustrated on any day when I haven't done something significant to help our country. That's my goal when I get up in the morning and that's my goal when the sun sets, and then some.

There's so much that needs to be done—help start a political action committee, encourage a candidate to run, write letters that motivate people and raise funds, bring key conservatives together to plan an important campaign, explain the New Right to a reporter or columnist, expand freedom in every possible way.

I was born in Golden Acres, Texas, right outside Houston, on September 23, 1933. My parents, Arthur and Elizabeth (nee Stoufflet), were of Louisiana French descent and moved to Texas the day they were married in August 1929, just before the Great Depression.

While the Viguerie family had some money and a great deal of real estate in South Louisiana, they lost just about everything in the financial panic of the early 1920's. Mother still retains a little of her Cajun accent. She spoke only French until she started school.

Dad had no college education (Mother had one year of college), and he went to work for the Shell Oil Co. as a construction worker. He was determined he wouldn't stay in the fields and he didn't. He worked his way up to top management.

Our family was thrifty. No money was ever wasted. My mother worked in a paper mill during World War II, doing a man's work. I suspect she actually did the work of several men. I remember we had a couple of cows, and I sold milk to the neighbors to bring in a little extra money for the family.

Dad usually worked two jobs—the one with Shell and the other hauling sand and gravel in a secondhand dump truck. We also had a vegetable garden and Mother and Dad canned vegetables for use during the winter. Of course Mother was keeping house and looking after me and my sister, Annette, so she had two jobs too.

My folks were old-fashioned, industrious people who believed in saving their money for a rainy day. They were conservative, but we didn't sit around the dinner table talking politics. They lived what they believed in, and that included God.

I went to public schools all my life except for 2/3 of a year at a Catholic school. I was a poor student in high school, but I was determined to attend college.

In January 1952, when I was 19, I went off to college —Texas A & I, in Kingsville, about 250 miles from Houston. I wanted to be an engineer. Why? Well, I had read that engineers were making a lot of money in South America so I figured I would make some quick money down south and come back to Houston—and run for Congress.

But, I had problems with algebra, so my teachers and I agreed I wasn't cut out to be an engineer. Well, I had observed that many politicians were lawyers. So I switched to pre-law.

In college, my big political heroes were "the two Macs"—Douglas MacArthur and Joseph McCarthy. I was very angry over the firing of MacArthur, who wanted to win the Korean war and beat the Communists.

And I felt the same way about Joe—he was a fighter fighting Communism. So I became a fighter. Even when he was inaccurate, McCarthy articulated my concern about a very big problem. There *are* Communists in this world. They are not the ghosts of a few rightwingers' imaginations.

While at Texas A & I, I joined a fraternity, Kappa Sigma, and became president in my last year there. Many of my buddies were veterans of the Korean War. The school had a Southern Baptist atmosphere and I was comfortable there. But I wanted to be close to the political action.

So, I switched schools in January 1956 to the University of Houston where I got my BS in political science with a minor in economics.

College was always very important to me. I knew it could open doors. Each summer, from the time I was 17, I worked at the refinery where my Dad worked, sometimes as a laborer. I dug ditches. I worked the midnight shift and the swing shift from 4 p.m. to midnight too. It was hard, exhausting work. Those summers were a strong incentive to finish college.

Still convinced that law was the road for me into politics, I enrolled in the University of Houston Law School. After 1½ semesters and a lot of C's and D's, I woke up to the fact that I was not going to be a second Clarence Darrow.

So I decided to get my military obligation out of the way. I enlisted in the U.S. Army Reserve program in March 1957, serving six months of active duty as an enlisted man and committing myself to another 7½ years in the reserves. I was stationed at Fort Chaffee, Arkansas.

As you can see, I was not exactly burning up the track and setting records. I was what you would call a late bloomer.

But I always knew I was going to do things, important things, that would make a big difference in people's lives.

And I knew I would do them through politics. Whenever I could make it, I was down at Republican headquarters, volunteering my time, working with the senior party, or with the Young Republicans.

I worked for Dwight Eisenhower in 1952 and 1956; I became chairman of the Harris County (Houston) Young Republicans. But I was always a conservative first.

I remember one time I invited Jack Cox, a big name Texas Democrat and a solid conservative, to speak at our YR barbecue. Several people strongly criticized the choice of a speaker since he was not a Republican. I was hurt and didn't understand their objections. We had a great turnout, hundreds of people, and Jack Cox made a stirring speech. Looking back on it, I see now I practiced coalition politics without realizing it.

About this time, I got a clerk's job in an oil company for $90 a week. I remember standing at the elevator one day and hearing somebody say that my boss's boss was making $150 a week. I found it hard to believe. I didn't think anyone his age could make that much money. I certainly didn't think I would, and I didn't care. I had plenty of politics to keep me busy in my spare time.

In 1960, as you know, Lyndon Johnson ran for vice president on the Democratic ticket with John F. Kennedy. What you may not remember is that Johnson also ran for reelection to the U.S. Senate from Texas that same year.

Tough little John Tower challenged LBJ, and we thought we had a chance if Nixon carried Texas and if enough people were upset at Johnson for running for two offices at the same time. We came up with a little slogan: "Double Your Pleasure, Double Your Fun—Vote Against LBJ Twice."

I was named Harris County campaign chairman for Tower and we put up a good fight. I did all the usual things, distributed literature, set up meetings, got out the vote. I also helped write a one-page fund raising letter for Tower that worked pretty well. I was kind of intrigued by it.

During the campaign, I heard that a group of young conservatives were meeting up north in Connecticut to form a national conservative youth organization, but I didn't go. I wasn't invited.

John Tower did very well that November—receiving 41% of the vote. It was a strong statewide showing for a Republican and a professor of economics who had never run for statewide office before. When Tower won the special senatorial election for LBJ's old seat in early 1961, I was not heavily involved.

After Tower was elected, I wanted to come to Washington with him in the worst way—as a mail room boy, as anything. I just knew that if I ever got the chance, good things would happen.

At last, in the summer of 1961, the opportunity came. And I did not hesitate. I guess you could say I got my break through a classified ad in *National Review*.

The ad said that a national conservative organization was looking for four field men. I checked it out with my friend David Franke, then with *National Review*, who told me the organization was Americans for Constitutional Action (ACA), an old-line conservative group founded in 1958. I was definitely interested.

I took a plane from Houston at midnight to save money and arrived in New York City at 4 a.m. I was as green as any kid who ever hit New York. I stood there at the east-side terminal with my suitcase. I was looking for a bus or cab to get to Dave Franke's apartment in Greenwich Village when I noticed these signs, "No Standing."

I wasn't 100% sure, but I didn't want to take any chances so I kept walking for blocks and blocks with the suitcase until I finally found Dave's apartment.

Later that morning I went uptown to *National Review*. I was about to cross East 35th Street when a man in a vested suit wearing a bowler hat and carrying an umbrella stopped me and said, "Mr. Viguerie, I presume?"

It was Bill Rusher, who took me inside the National Review building for the interview. It turned out to be not for a field position with ACA but for executive secretary of Young Americans for Freedom (YAF), the conservative youth organization to whose founding I had not been invited because none of the organizers had any reason to know who Richard Viguerie was.

Actually, the job was to be Marvin Liebman's account executive for the YAF account. It was up to the YAF board of directors to hire the executive secretary.

I hit it off well with everyone I met, especially Marvin Liebman, who was to teach me so much about direct mail. I went back to Houston the next day to wait, but not for very long. A call soon came that I was hired.

I had been dating a beautiful young lady, Elaine O'Leary, for six months. We decided to get engaged right away—at the San Jacinto Monument outside Houston, where Texas won its independence. A few weeks later, I was back in New York City.

I was surprised to learn after arriving on the job that YAF, not one year old, was $20,000 in debt with only a couple of weeks operating money in the bank. Having just received my big break in life, I wasn't about to have it disappear on me. I was determined that YAF would succeed.

Marvin suggested I call on various wealthy contributors and ask them for money. My first visit was to Gov. Charles Edison, youngest son of the great inventor Thomas Edison and former Secretary of the Navy and Governor of New Jersey.

I have rarely met a more charming, gracious, generous man. After making me feel comfortable (which was no small task), he wrote out a check for $500. YAF was to receive many more large checks from Governor Edison before he died in 1969.

Later I called or visited Captain Eddie Rickenbacker, J. Howard Pew and others. I was reasonably successful in persuading them to make sizeable contributions to YAF.

But I'm basically a pretty shy person and I did not feel comfortable asking for money directly. So I began writing letters instead, and they seemed to work. So I wrote more and more letters and before many months, direct mail was my whole focus—for fundraising, subscriptions for *The New Guard*, YAF membership, everything.

In November 1962, YAF moved to Washington, D.C., and Elaine and I moved with them. (We had been married in Houston in February 1962.) In early 1963, I asked the YAF board to hire David Jones, the Florida state YAF chairman, to be the executive director and let me concentrate exclusively on direct mail.

I did this until December 1964 when I decided to start my own direct mail company. By this time Elaine and I had a two-year old daughter, Reneé and a year-old daughter, Michelle. We had saved $4000. I took $400 from our savings and started the Richard A. Viguerie Company, Inc. in January 1965.

At the beginning, I had one employee and 12,500 names of contributors. We located on Capitol Hill, three blocks from Congress.

How did I get those contributor names? Simple. After November 1964, I went down to the office of the Clerk of the House of Representatives. They had on file—as required by law—the names and addresses of all those who had given $50 or more to the Goldwater campaign.

I copied down their names and addresses by hand until my fingers were numb. It was legal to copy such public records, and to use the names for advertising, but no photo-copying was allowed. After a couple of weeks, I hired several women to do the copying. We wound up with 12,500 conservative contributors—the beginning of my famous list, without which I wouldn't be in business today.

I do not recommend what I did then as the best way to start a new business. YAF was my only major client and within a few months I lost it. But other business soon came along.

Our first big political client was Sen. Robert Griffin of Michigan, who ran for a full term to the U.S. Senate in 1966. We wrote some very successful letters. It was like fireworks going off. Griffin won easily. I was surprised, and I still am surprised by what happens in this business. It's what makes it so exciting.

Gradually as the company developed and I learned more and more about direct mail, I began to understand my role in the conservative movement.

There were different routes I could have gone. We had outstanding writers, debaters and public speakers like Bill Buckley, Bill Rusher, Russell Kirk. I could have tried to go that route. And I probably wouldn't have amounted to a hill of beans. I didn't have the educational background, and I was starting too late to catch up with the others who had a 20-year head start.

But I realized that what we didn't have was someone who could take the ideas, the writings and the books and market them to the people.

When a new cause came along or a new candidate or a new organization, we didn't really have someone who understood how to market them on a national scale.

So I set out to become the best marketer I could be. I determined to learn how to successfully market ideas to millions. But it's not easy to learn a new profession at 30 years of age.

It was particularly hard for my wife, Elaine, in the early years. She not only took care of our two small children, but she handled most all the duties normally handled by the husband, such as repairs to the house and car, yard work, paying bills, etc.

This allowed me to spend as many as four hours a day studying direct mail in addition to holding down a full time job.

Also no one ever went to college to be a direct mail expert. In fact, most all direct mail executives that I know got into the business accidentally.

My first direct mail teacher was Marvin Liebman, who was during the 1950s and through the mid-60s the principal public relations, fund raising and direct mail expert for the conservative movement. Then he decided to move to London to try his hand at his first love—producing plays.

My next teacher was one of the great men of direct marketing, Edward N. Mayer, Jr. I first met Ed in May 1965 when I attended a direct mail seminar he was conducting. And for the next 11 years (until he passed away) he was my teacher and friend.

Occasionally someone will ask me to what I attribute my direct mail success. I'm sure there are a number of factors, but one of the most important is working long hours. Included in my 12-hour days, Monday through Friday (plus 10 hours on weekends), are 3 hours a day reading and studying direct mail. I only know a few people in political direct mail (with the exception of Viguerie Co. employees, of course) who have read more than three or four books on direct marketing.

And back in the 1960s, most politicians did not understand direct mail at all. However, I knew one liberal politician who definitely appreciated its importance. George McGovern called me in 1967 to ask if I would help with the direct mail fund-raising for his 1968 Senate race.

I explained to the Senator that we were poles apart ideologically and he'd want someone more akin with his philosophy. We had a good long chat. It was clear he had an appreciation of the power of direct mail.

In 1969, after his reelection, McGovern told liberal organizations and candidates he wanted to help them raise money. He was generous. He signed a lot of fund-raising letters. He wanted only one thing—the names and addresses of people who responded to those mailings.

So in January 1971, when George McGovern announced for President he had a tremendous head start—a mailing list of thousands of people who had responded to an appeal for contributions for liberal causes—primarily to end the Vietnam War.

In 1967, instead of McGovern, I became involved with Max Rafferty, who beat U.S. Sen. Tommy Kuchel, the

Republican minority whip, in the June 1968 GOP primary in California. It was a big upset, a phenomenal event. I feel it was done largely with direct mail.

We mailed twice to 2 million Republican households in California. I'm confident that the over 4 million letters we mailed to people in California was the major reason a relatively unknown state superintendent of education with little campaign money was able to beat one of California's best known and most powerful politicians by 67,000 votes.

In the November general election, they asked us to mail only to the 60,000 previous Rafferty contributors and used the money mostly to buy TV ads. They didn't want a big direct mail effort. While that wasn't the only reason Rafferty lost badly in November, I think it certainly was one of the principal reasons.

Because of this experience and others in which we raised a lot of money for causes or candidates who would spend the money in what I viewed as an ineffective way, I began to insist, starting around 1974, that the money we raised for the candidates through direct mail be used to send letters to voters in the candidates' district or state. The results have been good for the candidates and for the conservative movement.

Consider Phil Crane when he first ran for Congress from Illinois in a 1969 special election. He was one of 13 Republican primary candidates. If he won the primary, he would win the general because it was an overwhelmingly Republican district.

TV and newspaper advertising made little sense. His district was one of 14 districts covered by the Chicago mass media. Therefore, Phil needed to reach less than 5% of Chicago area citizens, the Republican voters in his district. Direct mail was the obvious medium to reach them.

We mailed two voter letters to every Republican in the district, and Phil Crane won in an upset. Just ten years later, Phil ran for the Republican nomination for President. He didn't win it but mark my words—he'll be back.

In 1971, I talked seriously to officials of the Committee to Re-Elect the President (CREEP). At the last minute we were denied the fund-raising account. Then they came back to us in late 1971 about doing Nixon voter mailings. But Kissinger had already gone to Peking and the Nixon administration was busy "tilting" toward Red China and leaning away from our old friend and ally, Taiwan.

In addition, Nixon had established wage and price controls and announced that he was a Keynesian in economics, was pushing to enlarge the welfare program, and in general appeared to be trying to impress the *Washington Post* and the *New York Times* editorial page writers with how modern and progressive he was.

I decided I wanted no part of Nixon.

Reflecting on it, I realize that Nixon may never have had any deep-rooted beliefs or goals, except those that furthered his particular personal ambition.

I remember in the 1968 campaign that Nixon spoke out strongly about the weapons imbalance between us and the Soviets. But when Humphrey charged hard in the very last days of the campaign, Nixon panicked and reversed a previous statement on the weapons issue. It hit me like a bolt of lightning. I said to myself, "That son of a gun really is sincerely, honestly tricky."

Because Nixon had moved to the left, I did the fundraising for Congressman John Ashbrook of Ohio when he ran against Nixon in 1972 for the Republican presidential nomination. I lost $250,000 on the Ashbrook campaign, which did not turn out to be a serious effort. There wasn't even a campaign manager after the Florida primary in March, although I lobbied hard for one. I saw clearly then that the people who were "leading" the conservative movement didn't understand how to lead.

I felt isolated and frustrated. I kept looking for people who could lead, who could make things happen. Finally, reluctantly, I began to call my own meetings.

I hosted one in December 1973 because I felt we were getting killed by Watergate. About 15 conservative Republican Congressmen attended a strictly private meeting. There was lots of talk, lots of suggestions, lots of smoke, but no fire. Nothing happened. They were afraid to act. They were impotent.

But as my wife Elaine likes to say, "When the good Lord closes a door he opens a window."

And who should come through the window and into my office in 1973, but the brother of George Wallace, who asked us to help the Governor retire his 1972 Presidential campaign debt.

We had doubts. They had reservations. Wallace was a Democrat and I was a Republican from that terrible place, Washington, D.C.

There were philosophical differences. Wallace was not a 100% conservative. He had a lot of populist, non-conservative ideas. But he and I agreed on about 80% of the important issues, social issues like busing and law and order, and the need for a strong national defense. So we struck a bargain.

I got a lot of criticism from old line conservatives. I was working for a prominent national Democrat—and national conservatives (until then) just didn't do things like that. Their negative reaction added to my growing disillusion with much of the established conservative leadership.

My working for Wallace—although I don't think I realized it at the time—was the beginning of my thinking in terms of coalition politics. I was encouraged by the fact that other conservatives like Paul Weyrich and Jeffrey St. John, the author and TV-radio commentator, were meeting and talking with Wallace. The three of us and our wives took a trip to Alabama to attend a social event at the Governor's Mansion in 1975. We were warmly received.

George Wallace was the first national candidate since Goldwater in 1964 that many conservatives strongly backed. We raised about $7 million for the Governor from 1973 through 1976. But I have to say that he disappointed me in that he never showed any interest in building a conservative movement.

Our efforts for Wallace were helped, believe it or not, by George McGovern, who had proven conclusively with his 1972 presidential race the power of direct mail. In fact, the person who suggested to the Wallace campaign that I be hired was Morris Dees, who did McGovern's direct mail in 1972, Carter's in 1976 and Kennedy's in 1980.

Another key factor in our growth was Watergate, which produced the Federal Election Campaign Act of 1974, limiting personal contributions to $1,000, per candidate per election.

Instead of turning to multi-millionaires like W. Clement Stone as Nixon did in 1972, presidential and all other federal candidates had to turn to the people. And there is no better way to get your message to the people and at the same time get them to give money than through direct mail.

I don't want to leave you with the impression that all of my clients are political candidates. Actually, less than 15% are. Many of our clients are what I call health and welfare clients.

But most are organizations with a conservative or right of center appeal. Our clients are concerned with issues such as gun control, pro-life, prayer in school, abuses by national union officials, wasteful government spending, high taxes, immorality on TV and in the movies, an educational system that can't educate, national defense and many other issues.

At the same time I'm proud of having helped elect fine conservatives like Jesse Helms, Strom Thurmond, Jim McClure, Orrin Hatch, Phil Crane, Mickey Edwards, Larry McDonald, Bob Livingston, Phil Gramm and Bob Dornan as well as helping effective conservative organizations like the National Right to Work Legal Defense Foundation, the National Rifle Association, *Human Events*, the American Security Council, The Conservative Caucus, the National Conservative Political Action Committee and dozens of others.

At present we have 250 employees, spread between The Viguerie Co. (including our computer installation), our mailing company and a list company. We also publish *Conservative Digest*, a monthly magazine for the New Majority, edited by John Lofton, one of the conservative movement's most talented writers, and *The New Right Report*, a twice a month newsletter, written by James Martin, one of the conservative movement's foremost direct mail advertising experts. In 1982, we plan to move into our own 100,000 square foot building in Northern Virginia.

It has not been an easy path. I'm usually at my desk by 7 a.m., Monday through Saturday. I usually eat my lunch at my desk or skip lunch. I bring home 10 to 12 hours of work on the weekends. This pace is less than it used to be, but I am always aware of what Winston Churchill once said: "So much to be done and so little time in which to do it."

I am deeply indebted to the employees of The Viguerie Company who make it possible for me to devote so much of my time and energy to the New Right.

They work long and hard and selflessly. Many times when I leave the office at 7 or 8 p.m., I'll pass five or six still working on a mailing whose deadline is fast approaching. A lot of people spend a lot of time making sure deadlines are met.

My success, such as it is, is not mine alone but a success based on the talent, experience and professionalism of hundreds of dedicated men and women, from executive vice president to file clerks.

By 1974 The Viguerie Co. was successful and well established. Elaine and I and our three children—Reneé, Michelle and Ryan—lived in a very comfortable home in Bethesda, Maryland. I should have been satisfied. I had come a very long way from the Houston oil refinery, a walk-up flat in Greenwich Village and a three-room office over Morton's Pharmacy on Capitol Hill.

But I knew I would never be happy until other conservatives and I came together and truly began saving our nation and the world from the liberal leaders and the liberal ideas which had almost destroyed us.

And so in 1973 and 1974, I began making new friends or reestablishing acquaintances with individuals who shared my concern and my frustration—people like Paul Weyrich, Morton Blackwell, Charlie Black, Howard Phillips, Bill Richardson, Woody Jenkins and others. We discovered that we all brought new things to the table.

Howard's idea was to go to the grassroots. Paul stressed precinct organization. Morton was my eyes and ears to the conservative movement, always insisting we pay attention to studying how to win and to the training of young people. Woody was a Louisiana Democrat who kept saying that not *all* the good guys were in the Republican Party.

Slowly but surely we came together. I'll never forget Morton telling me how shocked he was when he arrived in Washington as executive director of the College Republicans in the Sixties and discovered that Barry Goldwater, Strom Thurmond and John Tower didn't sit down each week to plan the conservative strategy for that week.

39

But without the battles which they won and lost, and those of many other conservatives in and out of Congress, we would have been forced to start almost from scratch. Instead, a solid foundation for the conservative movement had been built by solid men and women in the 1950's and 1960's.

V

The Foundations
of the New Right

Two men are more responsible than any other for the strength and vitality of conservatism in America today—Bill Buckley and Barry Goldwater.

Without them, an effective conservative movement might never have begun.

William F. Buckley, Jr., has played so many roles it's hard to name them all: Editor of *National Review*, the conservative intellectual journal for 25 years. Syndicated columnist since 1962 whose witty commentary has kept liberals off balance year after year. Host of the weekly TV program *Firing Line* since 1966, the only regular conservative show on the nation's most important mass medium. Author of a dozen-plus best-selling books, both fiction and non-fiction.

God and Man at Yale was published almost 30 years ago, in 1951. It was a literary shot heard around the nation, if not the world. And Bill has written so many other important books since then, not the least being his novels about a CIA agent named Blackford Oakes.

I ask you: Who else but Bill Buckley could write three best-selling books favorable to the CIA when that agency, unfortunately, has a reputation lower than a snake's belly?

Less well known, I'm sure, have been Bill Buckley's many organization contributions to the conservative movement. Young Americans for Freedom was founded at his family's Sharon, Conn., home in 1960. Over the next two years he helped the Conservative Party of New York, which has played such a decisive role in electing dozens of conservatives to the state legislature and the U.S. Congress.

Bill Buckley himself ran for mayor of New York City in 1965 in a memorable campaign. His effort is probably best remembered for his wisecrack response when he was asked what he would do if he won: "Demand a recount."

But in fact, in that race and elsewhere he proposed a number of sensible programs, prompting him later to write a small but important book, *Four Reforms*, which touched on welfare, taxes, crime and education.

Bill was a major figure in the 1964 founding of the American Conservative Union, which alone carried much of the organizational burden of the right until the mid-70's when New Right groups like The Conservative Caucus, the Committee for the Survival of a Free Congress and the National Conservative Political Action Committee were formed. He also worked closely with a number of anti-communist organizations in the 1950s and 1960s, including probably the best known of all—the Committee of One Million (Against the Admission of Communist China to the United Nations).

Through his wit, intelligence, and willingness to stand up for conservative principles, Bill Buckley, almost single-handedly, made the word "conservative" respectable and accepted.

Young people in today's climate may find it hard to believe, but in the mid-1950s when Bill Buckley started *National Review*, you did not shout your conservatism from the rooftops—you whispered it behind closed doors.

Particularly through *National Review*, he has helped develop some of our finest young conservative writers and thinkers—people like George Will, Joseph Sobran, George Nash, Neal Freeman, Richard Brookhiser and others.

It was Bill Buckley's unique contribution to draw together, basically through *National Review*, three kinds of conservatives in America. As outlined by George Nash in his definitive book, *The Conservative Intellectual Movement in America*, they were:

- The "classical liberals" or libertarians, who resisted the threat of government to liberty, free enterprise and the individual, including men like Frank Chodorov and John Chamberlain.

- The "new conservatives" or traditionalists, who urged a return to traditional religious and ethical standards, including men like Russell Kirk and Richard Weaver.

- The militant anti-communists, who believed that the West was engaged in a deadly struggle with communism, including men like Whittaker Chambers and James Burnham.

The New Right owes much of what we believe in and are fighting for to such outstanding men and the catalyst who brought them together, William F. Buckley, Jr.

Our debt to Barry Goldwater is as great. The Presidential campaign of 1964 was the first major political experience for most of us in the New Right.

As Paul Weyrich says, "Even if we did nothing but wear a Goldwater button or attend a rally—and some of the New Right are so young that is all they did—that campaign left an indelible mark on us."

You may remember some of the things Barry Goldwater said in his campaign—honest, true, blunt things. His words came back to haunt Americans in the aftermath of Vietnam, Agnew, Watergate, Nixon, and Carter.

Goldwater said in his 1964 campaign:

"There is violence in our streets, corruption in our highest offices, aimlessness among our youth, anxiety among our elders. . .

"Where examples of morality should be set, the opposite is seen. Small men, seeking great wealth or power, have too often and too long turned even the highest levels of public service into mere personal opportunity."

And he said:

"We have got to stop inventing ways to spend money and start thinking of ways to save some!

"Our growing revenue potential must be used to reduce taxes, eliminate perpetual deficits and repay debt, not to finance wasteful government spending or give the Administration in power even more power for political manipulation."

And he said:

"We (must) brand Communism as the principal disturber of peace in the world today—indeed, the only significant disturber of peace.

"We must make it clear that until its goals of conquest are absolutely renounced, and its relations with all nations tempered, Communism and the governments it now controls are enemies of every man on earth who is or wants to be free."

As Barry Goldwater said on January 3, 1964, when he announced his candidacy for the Republican nomination for President:

"I will offer a choice, not an echo."

27,174,898 Americans wanted that choice, and voted for the conservative Senator from Arizona on November 3, 1964.

Yes, it's true he lost badly, receiving only 39% of the vote and carrying only six states—Arizona and five Deep South states, Mississippi, Alabama, Louisiana, South Carolina and Georgia.

But it's also true that on the July day he was nominated, Senator Goldwater's own polls showed that only a little more than 20% of the electorate would vote for him. And as he writes in his autobiography, *With No Apologies:*

"In our public opinion samplings I was never more than 30 to Lyndon Johnson's 70 percent."

It was no small feat to double his poll position during a dirty campaign which included two TV commercials which pictured Barry Goldwater as a man who would bring nuclear death and destruction to the world.

Here is the *New York Times'* description of one TV spot: "A little girl licking an ice cream cone appeared on millions of television screens all over America. (A woman's voice) told her that people used to explode atomic bombs in the air and that the radioactive fallout made children die. The voice then told of a treaty preventing all but underground nuclear tests and how a man who wants to be President of the United States voted against it.

" 'His name is Barry Goldwater,' she said, 'so if he is elected, they might start testing all over again.' A crescendo of Geiger counter clicks almost drowned out the last words. Then came the male announcer's tag line: 'Vote for President Johnson on November 3rd. The stakes are too high for you to stay home.' "

And here is the *Times* report of the second TV commercial:

"A little girl with wind tossed hair was shown in a sunny field picking daisies. As she plucks the petals of one daisy, she counts. On the sound track, coming in stronger and stronger, a male voice counts backwards.

"When the girl reaches 10, the man's voice, in the doom-filled cadences of the countdown, reaches zero. The screen is rent by an atomic explosion.

" 'These are the stakes,' says the voice of Lyndon Baines Johnson. 'To make a world in which all of God's children can live, or go into the dark. We must either love each other, or we must die.'

"The doom-voice returns, urging viewers to vote for President Johnson on November 3rd: 'The stakes are too high for you to stay home.' "

It did not matter, as Senator Goldwater pointed out, that never once in any of his writings or his speeches did he advocate the use of military power to destroy Soviet Russia. What he did state repeatedly was that "the surest road to peace is through military strength."

Conservatives young and old learned a lot during the 1964 Presidential campaign. We learned how to stuff envelopes, ring doorbells, get out the vote on election day and contribute to a political campaign.

We also learned how to win a Presidential primary, how to select delegates to a national convention, how to put together a campaign team, how to use TV, radio and newspapers to communicate our message, how to go to the people at the grassroots for their help.

In fact, the Goldwater campaign of 1964 paved the way for the later successful use of direct mail by conservatives, especially the New Right.

For example, when Richard Nixon ran for President in 1960, individual financial contributors to his campaign probably ran between 40,000 and 50,000 people. In *The*

Conscience of a Majority, Senator Goldwater wrote: "The best count ever made of the individual contributions to my [Presidential] campaign. . .put the total at around 661,500."

Barry Goldwater also showed that it was possible to reach out and attract conservatives from every party and every walk of life. He wrote eloquently about these Americans way back on January 11, 1961:

"There are literally scores of millions of Americans who are either outside the organized pressure groups or find themselves represented by organizations with whose policies they disagree in whole or in part.

"These millions are the *silent Americans* who, thus isolated, cannot find voice against the mammoth organizations which mercilessly pressure their own membership, the Congress, and society as a whole for objectives which these silent ones do not want. They, thereby, have become the 'forgotten Americans' despite the fact that they constitute the majority of our people."

Barry Goldwater spoke for these silent, forgotten Americans in his 1964 Presidential campaign and in his many speeches and books, especially one, *The Conscience of a Conservative.*

It is, simply, the most popular political book in American history. Published in March 1960 by Victor Publishing, a small conservative firm, it has sold more than 3 million hardback copies and many millions of paperback copies.

In just 134 pages, *The Conscience of a Conservative* outlines a basic program for the preservation and extension of freedom in America and around the world. Its proposals for achieving economic strength at home and military strength abroad make just as much sense today as they did 20 years ago.

Which comes as no surprise to any conservative. Some things never change—like man's spiritual nature, the danger of a too powerful central government, Communism's persistent goal of wanting to bury us.

Barry Goldwater has been more than vindicated by the events of the 20 years since he wrote *The Conscience of a Conservative* and the 16 years since he ran for President of the United States. Conservatives owe him a debt which can never be adequately paid.

Although they have not played so prominent a role as Bill Buckley and Barry Goldwater, there are others who deserve to be mentioned for their important early contributions to the conservative movement.

• Frank Hanighen in 1944 founded *Human Events*, then a weekly newsletter, now a newspaper, which has consistently told conservatives what is really happening in Washington. Today, Tom Winter and Allan Ryskind continue to publish one of the best political newspapers in the country.

• In 1953, Russell Kirk wrote the classic book, *The Conservative Mind*, which provided a solid philosophical base for American conservatism.

• The same year, Frank Chodorov started the Intercollegiate Society of Individualists, now the Intercollegiate Studies Institute (ISI). Under the leadership of Victor Milione for the past 22 years, ISI has given conservative students books, seminars, publications and a sense of not being the only conservative in the world.

• Sen. Strom Thurmond of South Carolina has been a star in the conservative firmament for more than 30 years, contributing his time and talent again and again.

• Frank Meyer, author and senior editor of *National Review*, spent most of his life trying to "fuse" together the libertarian and traditionalist strains of the conservative movement. He was not only a writer but a doer, declaring that brave words without equally brave action meant very little.

• Ronald Reagan has helped raise millions of dollars for conservative organizations. Reagan's political involvement has offered hope for the future to thousands of conservative activists who thought of him as their political hero. This endorsement has helped give credibility to many conservative organizations including Young Americans for Freedom, American Legislative Exchange Council, National Conservative Political Committee and many others.

• Whittaker Chambers alerted countless Americans to the epic struggle between the Free World and communism through his moving book, *Witness*.

- Dr. Fred Schwarz of the Christian Anti-Communism Crusade put it as simply and persuasively as is possible with his classic work, *You Can Trust the Communists—To Be Communists.*

- Brent Bozell, as editor of the Catholic magazine, *Triumph,* and collaborator with Barry Goldwater on *The Conscience of a Conservative,* was one of the first conservatives to warn of the dangers of relying exclusively on the Republican Party.

- Milton Friedman spoke, wrote about and promoted conservative economics so brilliantly that they finally had to give him a Nobel Prize.

- Walter H. Judd, a former Congressman, medical missionary and staunch anti-communist, was the driving force behind one of the very first conservative single issue groups—The Committee of One Million, launched in 1953.

- John Fisher founded the American Security Council in 1955 and has built it into the most active pro-national defense organization in the country.

- M. Stanton Evans, as author of YAF's Sharon Statement, newspaper editor, TV and radio commentator, former chairman of the American Conservative Union and now head of the ACU Education and Research Institute and its Washington Journalism Center, has been a major architect of American conservatism.

These are just some of the dedicated conservatives who helped lay the foundation for one of the most dramatic developments in modern American politics—the birth of the New Right.

By the early 1970's, many of us (Paul Weyrich, Howard Phillips, Morton Blackwell, and others) were working in the Nation's Capital. We met informally from time to time, at a luncheon or at a social function, to talk conservative politics. Occasionally, we worked together to help a rising conservative—like Congressman Jim McClure when he ran for and won a Senate seat from Idaho in 1972.

But there was no organized, continuing effort to exert political influence on elections, on Capitol Hill, on the news media and on the nation at large.

It was almost as though we were waiting for a challenge which would force us to test our strength and our convictions. And one day, something did happen which so angered us that we resolved to fight back as hard as we knew how. We haven't stopped fighting since.

VI

The Birth of the New Right

One morning in August 1974, I turned on my television to watch our brand-new President Gerald Ford announce he was picking Nelson Rockefeller to be his vice president.

Nelson Rockefeller! The liberal who attacked Barry Goldwater during the GOP primaries in 1964 so strongly it helped defeat Goldwater in November. The liberal who got Richard Nixon to agree to the infamous midnight Pact of Fifth Avenue in 1960, placing a liberal stamp on the GOP platform. Nelson Rockefeller—the high-flying, wild-spending leader of the Eastern Liberal Establishment.

As a conservative, I could hardly have been more upset if Ford had selected Teddy Kennedy.

After all, there were a number of good conservatives Ford could have picked, starting with Ronald Reagan and Barry Goldwater. But Jerry Ford revealed the true colors of so-called "moderate" Republicanism by choosing the very symbol of everything we conservatives had always opposed.

I immediately got on the phone and invited about 14 conservative friends to dinner the next night to talk about how we could stop Rockefeller from becoming vice president.

We were an assortment of political activists, Capitol Hill aides, journalists, a lawyer or two, leading Washington conservatives. We came up with a few good ideas, but I soon realized the conservatives didn't have the leadership or the clout to stop Nelson Rockefeller from becoming the next vice president. And we quickly learned that most Republicans, while not enthusiastic about Rockefeller and even preferring Reagan or Goldwater, had no stomach for a hard-nosed fight so soon after Richard Nixon's resignation.

As they had so often in the past, most Republicans chose to put party before principle.

Well, we didn't stop Rocky. And I realized that we might be close to losing the entire battle to the Left unless some of us who had not previously taken a leadership role stepped out front and center. That night in August it became clear to me that the conservatives were in desperate need of leadership.

I decided to give up some of the time I was spending with my family, and on the golf course, and spend that time helping to organize the movement. In short, I decided to stop following and start doing some leading of my own.

There were, of course, other factors beside the Rockefeller nomination which brought us together.

Some of us, like Howard Phillips, had been an important part of the Nixon administration. Howard had waged a three-year campaign to secure permission from the Nixon administration to abolish the Office of Economic Opportunity (OEO), and its programs.

Buoyed by the promise of a Nixon veto of any OEO funding after June 30, 1973, he set out to do just that. Then as Richard Nixon became more and more preoccupied with Watergate, liberal White House staffers decided OEO dismantlement was too controversial. They decided instead to continue and even expand OEO programs.

In mid-1974, Howard and I started Conservatives for the Removal of the President—CREEP II. We were afraid Nixon would make concessions to the Russians as he tried to deal with Watergate. I had known Howard from the early days of YAF and admired his energy, brains and determination.

Others had been disillusioned by Spiro Agnew's fall. Conservatives had applauded Agnew's attacks on liberal hypocrisy and elitism in the news media and elsewhere. They felt Agnew had given voice to the Silent Majority. But he turned out to be all too willing to compromise himself and his office for a few dollars.

Others of us were tired of losing. The old right many times gave the appearance they believed that being right was enough—and should determine the battle's outcome. Also, because they had been fighting liberalism since the 1930s, older conservatives tended to be defensive and defeatist. They spent so much time putting out liberal fires, they had little time to start any fires of their own.

Others of us were just plain impatient. These young conservatives were ambitious, aggressive, coming into their prime. They were tired of sitting around and waiting for older conservatives to start leading.

I would have preferred then as now to have stayed home with my wife and children, be on the golf course and/or be in my office tending to my direct mail business, but there was work to be done.

And I think that most of my associates in the conservative movement would also prefer to be home with their families rather than in early morning and late night meetings, airports, hotel rooms, making speeches to strangers, living out of a suitcase, etc.

Why have we taken up the challenge? Because there are people dying and suffering at the hands of brutal dictators. There are people who are slaves to drugs, or without jobs, or not eating, or going out of business, and in numbers never dreamed of before, all because of government failures and interference.

The liberals and the socialists have had their opportunity to try and help people. But ironically, almost all the problems in the world have gotten much worse since the liberals took control of the world's most influential and powerful nations.

Basically we on the New Right had four things in common:

1. A developing technical ability—in direct mail, in mass media, in practical politics.

2. A willingness to work together for the common good.

3. A commitment to put philosophy before political party.

4. An optimism and a conviction that we had the ability to win and to lead America.

We didn't call ourselves the New Right, at least not right away. The term was first used in a different context by Lee Edwards in 1962 when he proposed a conservative platform for Young Americans for Freedom in an article in *The New Guard*. The article was entitled: "The New Right: Its Face and Future."

Conservative columnist M. Stanton Evans used the phrase in 1969 to describe the emerging conservatism on college campuses—contrasting the New Right with the New Left then getting so much publicity.

But political columnist and analyst Kevin Phillips was the first, in 1975, to use the term in talking about "social conservatives" and the first to use it in regard to the collective efforts of Paul Weyrich, Howard Phillips, Terry Dolan, myself and others.

The more we talked and worked and planned together, the more we realized we could make things, important things, happen. We learned together and we helped educate each other about movement building. And the man perhaps with the broadest vision was Paul Weyrich. I can think of no one who better symbolizes or is more important to the conservative movement than Paul Weyrich.

He started or played the critical role in such key conservative groups as the Heritage Foundation, the American Legislative Exchange Council, the Republican Study Committee, the Senate Steering Committee, Library Court, to name a few. He and Howard Phillips spent countless hours with electronic ministers like Jerry Falwell, James Robison and Pat Robertson, urging them to get involved in conservative politics.

Many influential people are involved in major conservative activities because Paul recognized their potential and sought them out. He has probably spent several thousand hours in one-on-one meetings, urging influential people to get involved.

Paul's success is based on three things: (1) His absolute integrity—he is totally dedicated to conservative principles, (2) His absolute reliability. If he makes a commitment, he holds to it, no matter what, and (3) His brain. Paul is one of the most intelligent and perceptive people I have ever met.

Paul remembers the day he decided to switch from supporting conservative leaders to becoming one himself. He had been working as an aide to Sen. Gordon Allott of Colorado, a solid Republican conservative, for several years.

One day, during the first Nixon administration, he sat in on a meeting of top liberals planning to push through enactment of an open housing bill. Present were a high White House official (appointed by Nixon but a certified liberal), a columnist for a Washington newspaper, someone from the Brookings Institution, representatives from various black pressure groups and aides to a dozen key senators.

"They planned their campaign in a very impressive way," remembers Paul. The Senate aides committed their bosses to make statements and contact other senators. The White House official promised to keep track of the Administration's actions. The columnist said he would write a favorable article. The Brookings man promised to publish a study in time to affect the debate. The blacks agreed to provide street demonstrations at the right moment.

"I saw how easily it could be done," recalls Paul, "with planning and determination, and decided to try it myself." And he has, very successfully.

In 1974, with the financial help of business leader Joseph Coors and at my own strong urging, Paul Weyrich founded the Committee for the Survival of a Free Congress (CSFC). My company was more than willing to do the direct mail advertising. CSFC wasted no time in making a difference.

Less than four years later, in 1978, CSFC spent $400,000 to help elect 31 conservative candidates, including Senators Gordon Humphrey, Roger Jepsen, Bill Armstrong and John Warner, as well as Congressmen Jim Jeffries, Bill Carney, Ken Kramer, Jerry Solomon and Wayne Grisham.

Paul preaches the gospel of organization, insisting that campaigns he supports be well-organized.

"In the past," he says, "many of our conservative candidates ran strictly issue-oriented campaigns but didn't adopt many of the technical operations necessary to win."

Paul is very high on the "Kasten Plan" (named after Senator Robert Kasten), by which a specific voter turnout goal is set for every precinct in the Congressional district and a precinct chairman is given the responsibility of meeting this goal.

CSFC sponsors week-long schools, covering all the elements of a campaign, including surveys, the media, opposition research, precinct organization, recruitment and coalition building. At the week's end, teams are pitted against each other in a simulated election.

"You really find out from the results who has learned from the school and who has not," he notes.

Paul looks for and supports candidates who have a winning attitude. "If a candidate comes in here and says, 'Well, I don't think I can win, but boy, I think I can run a good race,' he doesn't get our help. We want candidates who say, 'By golly, we can lick this guy, and here's how we're going to do it, and every waking moment of my life and that of my family is going to be spent toward that objective.' "

Paul typifies the political philosophy of the New Right which parallels the military philosophy of Douglas MacArthur, "There is no substitute for victory."

In fact, Paul likes to argue that we are at war. "It may not be with bullets," he concedes, "and it may not be with rockets and missiles, but is is a war nevertheless. It is a war of ideology, it's a war of ideas, it's a war about our way of life. And it has to be fought with the same intensity, I think, and dedication as you would fight a shooting war."

Paul is constantly looking for new groups to add to the growing New Right coalition—anti-abortion groups, veterans groups, religious groups, tax groups, small businessmen, etc. He believes that family-oriented issues will be the key issues of the 1980s. He is, for example, president of the Free Congress Research and Education Foundation, which has a Family Policy Division specializing in such issues.

He compares the New Right to the "brain trust" that came in with Franklin Delano Roosevelt when he was first elected in 1932 (11 years before Paul Weyrich was born).

"We are radicals," he says, "who want to change the existing power structure. We are not conservatives in the sense that conservative means accepting the status quo.

"We cannot accept the status quo. Today isn't the same as the 1950s when conservatives were trying to protect what was, consitutionally, economically and morally, in the control of more or less conservative people."

Today's establishment, he declares, is in the hands of liberals who must be resisted and then replaced.

Liberals came up with giving away the Panama Canal, he argues.

Liberals have put us in a second rate military position through a failure to develop new weapons and via one-sided treaties like SALT I.

Liberals want to spend so much money that the future of our children is already mortgaged.

It is liberals who want the federal government to intervene in nearly every aspect of our lives.

"We have to take a turn in the other direction," Paul asserts. "The New Right does not want to conserve, we want to change—we *are* the forces of change. And if people are sick and tired ot things in this country, then they had best look to conservative leadership for that change."

To leaders, for instance, like 30-year-old John (Terry) Dolan, chairman of the National Conservative Political Action Committee (NCPAC). Founded in 1975 by young conservatives Charles Black, Roger Stone and Terry Dolan, NCPAC has become the largest conservative PAC in the country. It distributed over $2.3 million in cash and in-kind contributions to political races in 1980. It spent millions of dollars more in other areas, such as advertising, to elect conservatives. I'm proud to say that my company has handled the direct mail for NCPAC.

Terry himself helped engineer the revolutionary 1978 successful senatorial campaign of Gordon Humphrey, which used Boston radio and TV for the first time in a major way to reach the New Hampshire voters. Under his guidance, NCPAC has made a specialty of participating in primaries, believing that a well-placed dollar in a primary campaign which is usually poorly organized and under-financed, has more clout than in a general election, when more money and organization are generally available.

NCPAC relies heavily on research and polling, a reflection of one of its founders, conservative pollster Arthur Finkelstein. The committee works not only in federal but in state and local campaigns where again a modest amount of money or organization can make a big difference.

NCPAC has pioneered in what is called the "independent expenditure campaign"—in which a political action committee may legally spend as much as it wants for or against a candidate so long as there is no contact whatsoever between the PAC and the candidate and his organization.

For example, a PAC called Anybody But Church could legally spend $5 million or whatever it could raise to help elect Steve Symms to the U.S. Senate as long as none of the PAC's leadership was in contact in any way with Symms or his staff. Or the same PAC could spend millions attacking Frank Church—again as long as it was not coordinating its efforts in any way with the Symms campaign.

In 1978, NCPAC ran independent expenditure ads in Iowa, Colorado and Kentucky, attacking Senators Dick Clark, Floyd Haskell and Walter Huddleston for supporting the Panama Canal treaties—ads which contributed to the defeat of Clark and Haskell. In 1980 NCPAC sponsored advertising campaigns against six of the most liberal U.S. Senators—George McGovern of South Dakota, Frank Church of Idaho, John Culver of Iowa, Birch Bayh of Indiana, Thomas Eagleton of Missouri and Alan Cranston of California. All but the last two were defeated.

Here is just one anti-McGovern TV spot which will give you an idea of how NCPAC drives the liberals crazy:

"Globetrotter is a great name for a basketball team.

"But it's a terrible name for a senator.

"Only one senator did more globetrotting last year than George McGovern.

"While the energy crisis was brewing, George McGovern was touring Cuba with Fidel Castro. He also took a one-month junket to Africa. All at taxpayer's expense."

Terry Dolan is busy on many different conservative battlegrounds. He is chairman of the Washington Legal Foundation, as well as Conservatives Against Liberal Legislation (CALL), a lobbying group.

What Paul Weyrich is to the conservative movement in Washington, D.C., 39-year-old Howard Phillips is to the grassroots movement around the country.

Howard is founder and national director of The Conservative Caucus, launched in 1975, which now has 300,000 contributors and supporters, chairmen in 250 Congressional districts and an annual budget of almost $3 million. Again, my company was happy to undertake the direct mail advertising program for the Caucus at the beginning and continuing to this day.

The Conservative Caucus' basic goal is to mobilize a Congressman's constituents so as to influence his legislative record and thereby national policy.

"We have three basic jobs," Howard explains: to recruit and train local leaders, to lobby at the grassroots level, and to help set the agenda for national debate, by emphasizing the conservative viewpoint on key issues like the Panama Canal, SALT II and Communism in Central America.

"I firmly believe that right now, if we fight only at the national level, we lose. But using our strength at the local level, at the grassroots, we can win. And we have.

"If it had not been for the 50-state campaign of The Conservative Caucus and the SALT Syndrome film of the American Security Council, SALT II might have passed the U.S. Senate in the summer of 1979."

The Caucus' sister organization is The Conservative Caucus Research, Analysis and Education Foundation, a tax-deductible organization, which publishes *Congressional Report*, *Senate Report* and *Senate Roll Call*, maintains an active Speakers Bureau and a Legislative Data Bank.

Recently, The Foundation initiated a Research Bureau program to monitor federal departments and agencies. In 1979, it sponsored the Religious Roundtable, which has become a major educational force in briefing religious leaders on public policy issues.

"Conservatives," insists Howard, "must establish ourselves first as the opposition, then the alternative, finally the government."

The New Right, he says, was born out of Watergate.

"Many of us used to believe that conservative fortunes were synonymous with Republican fortunes. We placed an inordinate hope in the GOP and in Richard Nixon.

"Because many key GOP Congressmen and Senators were so personally fond of Richard Nixon, they frequently acquiesced in liberal policies, simply because Nixon was their advocate. Watergate changed that."

Another key leader is Morton Blackwell, described by *Human Events* as "the eyes and ears" of the New Right. Before joining Sen. Gordon Humphrey's staff in mid-1979 as policy director, Morton was chairman of the Committee for Responsible Youth Politics (CRYP), editor of *The New Right Report* and a key executive of my company for seven years. He is a contributing editor to *Conservative Digest*, organizer of an informal bi-weekly luncheon meeting of conservative PAC leaders and president of the Leadership Institute, which trains young people in leadership techniques. At 41, he is a major figure in the New Right and liaison among the various elements of the Washington conservative community.

After the Reagan victory, Morton, who oversaw the 1980 Youth For Reagan effort, served in the Presidential Personnel office of the Office of the President Elect.

Through CRYP and the Leadership Institute, Morton has recruited and trained literally thousands of young men and women, hundreds of whom now hold responsible positions in the conservative movement at national, state and local levels.

Graduates of Morton's training include Terry Dolan of the National Conservative Political Action Committee; Henry Walther, vice president and director of membership services for the National Right to Work Committee and a top New Right leader; Steve Markman, legislative assistant to Sen. Orrin Hatch; Baker Smith, executive director of the tax-deductible Center on National Labor Policy; Bill Olson, chairman of the Fairfax County (Va.) Republican Committee; Chris Lay, legislative assistant to Senator Steve Symms; Steve Antosh, legislative assistant to Senator Don Nickles; Bob Lauterberg, staff member of the House Republican Study Committee, and John Maxwell, campaign manager for both the victorious Chuck Grassley and Roger Jepsen Senate campaigns in Iowa.

Morton is optimistic but realistic about the future.

"Conservatives have reached the point," he has said, "where we are competitive in political races almost anywhere in the United States. We have reached the point where we can stop a significant percentage of the bad legislation.

"We are living in an environment," Morton continued, "where the issues that are taken up are not in our hands. The opposition picks the agenda, and we have to react to it. Until we take one or both of the Houses of Congress, the actual formation of the agenda is going to be out of our hands."

He was speaking before November, 1980. We are now rapidly approaching the point where we can pass legislation we would like to have passed, or repeal legislation we would like to see off the books.

Morton is proud of CRYP for having led the way in something that most New Right organizations now insist on—developing their own program of leadership training. He is also typical of New Right leaders who not only plan ahead but analyze what has happened—after the victory or the defeat. And he is a great sharer of ideas and knowledge. Among the New Right, there is a constant cross-fertilization of expertise and information.

Looking ahead to the 1980s, Morton sees larger numbers of conservative movement candidates, and far more technologically proficient candidates.

"They're starting earlier," he reports, "hiring their staff, their pollsters, their media consultants. They're starting earlier to gather the lists of their friends and associates to get them to pledge and work in their campaigns. The candidates who are smart are on the phone early to the national leaders of conservative organizations whether they're broad spectrum groups or focused issue groups."

And invariably, they'll be in touch with Morton Blackwell to find out where to go and whom to see.

And so, starting in 1974, we worked long and hard to build a new conservative movement. We were far from perfect. We made mistakes. In 1976, we backed some losing candidates, but also key winners like Orrin Hatch, Mickey Edwards and Bob Dornan.

But on the balance we had impact. We learned by our mistakes and we weren't afraid to make mistakes. We began to be noticed. We were written up in the national media and torn down by nervous liberals.

Here's an example of how we made them not only nervous but worried.

In March of 1977, Jimmy Carter proposed four changes in our election laws.

They would: (1) have the taxpayers finance all Congressional elections; (2) allow any voter to vote on election day if they showed up with most any kind of identification; (3) change the Hatch Act to allow Federal employees to actively participate in politics; (4) change the U.S. Constitution to allow for the direct election of the President and do away with the electoral college.

A few weeks later at about 10:15 one night, my phone rang. It was Paul Weyrich.

He said he had just attended a meeting of conservative Republican Senators. He said they had come to the conclusion that even though these election law changes would hurt the Republican Party, there was nothing they could do to stop it—most felt that they were ideas whose time had come.

I told Paul that I felt the New Right could develop the strategy to stop Carter's plan.

I also reminded Paul that it was late, that he had awakened me and that I would call him in the morning.

I called him the next morning, and we decided to have a meeting once a week in my conference room with about 15 key New Right leaders.

We quickly developed our strategy. Then week after week (sometimes we met more than once a week) we developed and implemented our tactics.

We made mailings to large Republican contributors, asking them to call wavering Senators. We arranged for Op-Ed pieces in major newspapers. We held briefings with the press to explain our position. We mailed millions of letters, asking that phone calls, cards and letters be sent to Congress.

We also used smart public relations wherever we could.

For example, Congressman Steve Symms and Robert Dornan got national coverage in July 1977 with dummy ID cards (the brainstorm of Dick Dingman at a meeting in my conference room) to demonstrate the possibilities for fraud in Carter's instant voter registration plan.

The ID cards each had the photos of either Symms or Dornan but the names of liberal Democrats on the House Administration Committee who supported Carter's plan. The reporters and the photographers loved it, particularly when liberal Committee Chairman Frank Thompson blew his top in public over the ID's.

The *Washington Star* published an enormous five-column photo on page one of the phony ID's, which had been blown up to poster size for a news conference.

On that day, Carter's plan to let anyone vote who turned up at the polls with just about any kind of paper showing he lived in that voting district died and has not been heard from since.

The liberal National Committee For An Effective Congress was opposed to one portion of the campaign finance bill, and Common Cause opposed Carter's proposed changes in the Hatch Act. So we worked with both of these liberal organizations in the area that concerned them.

Senator Paul Laxalt worked with many businessmen to urge them to pressure Congress.

Laxalt agreed to coordinate the effort inside the Senate. He organized and led a successful filibuster that for weeks defeated the best efforts of President Carter, Senate Majority Leader Bobby Byrd, Teddy Kennedy and other liberals to pass taxpayer financing of Congressional elections. And on August 2, 1977 the liberals threw in the towel.

This was the New Right at its best.

About 50 of us got together in September, 1977 at a dinner in Washington to celebrate David's victory over Goliath.

Despite four years of Carter efforts to change the election laws to put the conservatives out of business, not one of his changes has been passed.

This was probably the first major victory of the New Right. A rag-tag group of New Right conservatives had done what Republican Senators said could not be done.

We had our first taste of victory. And there was no stopping us now.

U.S. News & World Report said about us in July 1977: "A third force is quietly building a political apparatus that pointedly disregards party labels."

The *New York Times* said in December 1977: "The New Right . . . is more tightly organized, better financed, more sophisticated and more pragmatic than their predecessors."

Eddie Mahe, then executive director of the Republican National Committee, commented in June 1977: "If you ranked political institutions in this country, organized labor would be first. The Democratic Party is second. The Republican Party is third. [The New Right] is unquestionably fourth."

Lyn Nofziger, Assistant to the President for Political Affairs: "The old right were talkers and pamphleteers. They would just as soon go down in flames as win. But the New Right has moved toward a more pragmatic goal of accomplishing things."

One of the major differences in this group of new conservatives was that we weren't afraid to try even if there was only a 20% chance of success.

We weren't worried about how the establishment, the press and others would view us if we lost. We knew if you expected to hit a lot of home runs, you had to expect to strike out a lot.

Remember that in 1927, when Babe Ruth led the major leagues with 60 home runs, he also led in strikeouts with 89.

Between 1974 and 1978, the New Right received a lot of criticism from other conservatives who felt that we were wasting our time and dividing the resources of the conservative movement by moving in new directions and starting new publications, new political action committees, new research foundations, and new public interest law firms. They were greatly concerned about our massive use of technology such as computerized direct mail.

We have won by being firm and aggressive. Our language at times makes more gentle sorts nervous. But this is the way of most all successful political movements.

It's easy to complain about this or that thing that the New Right has done. In fact, there are lots of things we've done that we would do differently now, things we'd like to retract, words we'd like to pull back.

But to those conservatives who complain about mistakes the New Right has made, I ask, "Would you prefer that conservatives go back to the way we did things 10 years ago?"

Those few who complain and like to highlight our shortcomings remind me of the story about the man whose car motor stopped at the traffic light. When the light turned green, he still couldn't get the car started and the man next in line started honking his car horn. After a minute or so of this, the man whose motor wouldn't start got out of his car and went to the man sitting in the car behind him who was honking.

And he suggested that they change jobs. He said, "I'll honk your horn, and you go start my car."

Those who feel they could do it better, let them step forward. I for one will gladly turn over my pressure cooker-type life, 12-hour days, 70-hour weeks to anyone who can be more effective.

But unless you've shown that you know how to take control of this country from Big Media, Big Business, Big Labor, Big Government, then show a little patience with and understanding for those who have proven that they just might be able to do it.

While almost no one (myself included) likes to be criticized, especially unfairly and by those with whom you share a common goal, we were convinced we were doing the right thing.

We also knew that if we were successful, few would remember the criticism and the negative media coverage. If we were unsuccessful, we felt freedom in America and around the world would be reduced and even lost.

All the while, the pressure on us to perform more and more effectively became greater and greater.

By late 1977, the liberals had clearly picked their strategy to try to finish us off. They said that if the New Right didn't come up with a couple of really big wins in 1978, we would be exposed as all smoke and no fire.

But we were ready, and confident. And 1978 *was* a crucial turning point in the history of the New Right, and perhaps in our nation's history as well. Ironically, our greatest victories came as a result of a battle we lost—the Panama Canal treaties.

VII

1978: Our Critical Year

No political issue in the last 25 years so clearly divided the American establishment from the American people as the Panama Canal treaties.

In favor of the treaties were the Carter administration, the Democratic leadership in both Houses of Congress, both living ex-Presidents (six U.S. Presidents helped negotiate the treaties), Big Labor, Big Business, Big Media, the big international banks, and just about every liberal political and cultural star you could name.

Against the treaties were the American people—about 70% of them, according to the polls. Probably over 85% of registered Republicans opposed the giveaway of the Panama Canal.

And yet, the Republican Party refused to take the leadership in opposing the treaties. So the New Right picked up the flag and set out to do battle with the American establishment.

In November 1977, I said publicly that the Panama Canal was a "no-loss" issue for conservatives. I predicted that it would not only rally conservatives but bring countless members of the Silent Majority into the conservative movement. I called the Canal "the most electrifying issue conservatives have ever had."

Ronald Reagan made the Canal a major issue during the 1976 Republican Presidential primaries, declaring: "The Canal is ours. We built it. We paid for it. And we intend to keep it."

And the Panama Canal in turn saved Reagan from certain defeat. Governor Reagan appeared not to be a viable presidential candidate after his defeat in the 1976 Florida and New Hampshire primaries.

Then two things happened: (1) Sen. Jesse Helms and his longtime political adviser Tom Ellis took over the running of Reagan's primary campaign in North Carolina and (2) Reagan decided to make the Panama Canal a major issue between himself and President Ford. As a result, he won the North Carolina primary, got back on the offensive and almost won the Presidential nomination.

Other conservative spokesmen detailed the strategic importance of the Canal—the Marxist commitment of Panamanian dictator Omar Torrijos—the $10 billion investment of the American people in the Canal—and the importance of the Canal as a preeminent symbol of America's "can-do" spirit.

As columnist Patrick J. Buchanan wrote in January 1978:

"The Panama Canal is the right issue at the right time in the right place to say, 'This far and no farther.' A political war to the death over the Canal treaty could realign American politics, reinvigorate a weakened spirit of nationalism, and if lost, do for those who surrendered the Canal what Yalta did for the Democratic Party."

Exactly what we had in mind.

The Left won the Senate vote on the Panama Canal. But it was a very costly battle and it may be a major factor in their losing the war.

At the heart of the campaign was the close cooperation between anti-treaty forces in the U.S. Senate (the "inside" team) and forces generating grassroots opposition to the treaties (the "outside" team). The key man was Sen. Paul Laxalt of Nevada, whose competence and composure under pressure won respect on all sides.

Laxalt held frequent meetings—which became daily as the battle warmed up—at which anti-treaty Senators, New Right leaders Paul Weyrich, Howard Phillips and Terry Dolan, public relations expert William Rhatican, representatives of the Senate Steering Committee and other New Right leaders would decide the best tactics to win over undecided Senators.

At the same time, the "outside" team was carrying out the most intense issue-oriented political campaign in our nation in a decade. We wound up coordinating our activities with nearly 20 national organizations, an exercise in coalition building none of us will ever forget.

There were endless brainstorming sessions about the best approach to each undecided Senator, which mailing lists to use against which Senator, which primary or general election challenger of a pro-treaty Senator to encourage.

Terry Dolan decided that NCPAC would write 10,000 leading Republicans urging them to tell Howard Baker that a pro-treaty vote would ruin his presidential hopes.

Information was made available to State Rep. Woody Jenkins of Louisiana, whose major U.S. Senate primary effort helped force incumbent Democrat J. Bennett Johnston to vote against the treaties.

Those were long days and long nights. Some would begin with an 8 a.m. breakfast at my home in McLean, Va., and end at 10 p.m. with a leadership meeting somewhere else in the Washington area. Thousands of telephone calls, including scores of conference calls, were made at all hours.

Raw numbers will give you some idea of our efforts. The Conservative Caucus under Howard Phillips mailed 3 million letters and conducted anti-treaty rallies and campaigns in all 50 states. Terry Dolan's National Conservative Political Action Committee sent out almost half a million letters.

John Fisher's American Security Council mailed 2 million letters. The Council on Inter-American Security, under Ronald Docksai and L. Francis Bouchey, mailed 2 million letters, and broadcast radio spots in 13 states.

The American Conservative Union's half-hour TV documentary on the Panama Canal reached an estimated 10 million viewers, and raised $1 million. ACU also mailed 2 million letters.

And a "Truth Squad" featuring Senators Paul Laxalt, Jake Garn and Bill Scott, Congressmen Phil Crane, Larry McDonald and Mickey Edwards, and two dozen other political and military leaders reached over 10 million

Americans through TV and newspaper coverage of their appearances in key states.

I volunteered to raise the money for the Truth Squad. We mailed 5,000 letters and raised over $110,000. Several conservative groups also contributed $5,000 each, including The Conservative Caucus, the American Security Council, the Committee for the Survival of a Free Congress, National Conservative Political Action Committee, Citizens for the Republic, the American Conservative Union, and the Richard A. Viguerie Company.

This money was used to finance a chartered Boeing 737 jet, broadcast radio ads on the status of undecided Senators, run newspaper ads and distribute information about the Canal.

The Truth Squad trip in late January and early February 1978 was organized by Bill Rhatican and resembled a White House campaign trip. The travelling party, which covered more than 6,000 miles in less than four days, included 30 representatives of the national news media.

There were major news conferences at each of the four stops—Miami, St. Louis, Denver and Portland, Ore.—and each time conservatives received excellent local and national coverage.

The Truth Squad trip was a prime example of how conservatives were learning invaluable lessons in the political major leagues—lessons which we would put to good use later in 1978.

A few months earlier, Phil Crane, Rich Williamson and I decided that we needed a good readable book on the Panama Canal. I agreed to publish it. And so in January 1978, 100,000 paperback copies of *Surrender in Panama* by Congressman Philip M. Crane came out. Copies were sent to just about every important media person and political leader in the country. It was another example of how the New Right operates when it goes into high gear.

While all this was going on, the Republican National Committee was mailing out millions of letters signed by Ronald Reagan asking people to contribute to the RNC in an effort to defeat the Panama Canal treaties. Approximately $700,000 was raised.

But when Paul Laxalt asked RNC Chairman Bill Brock for $50,000 to help underwrite the cost of the Truth

Squad, the RNC chairman refused. The outrageous fact is that Brock refused to spend any of the money raised by Reagan's anti-treaty letter on any anti-treaty activities.

At their insistence, Laxalt and Reagan talked with Brock on December 15, 1977 via a joint telephone call and came away very angry. Brock would not budge. Someone present during this conversation said he heard Reagan use words that he didn't know Reagan knew.

Almost immediately, Senator Laxalt and Congressman Phil Crane, then chairman of the American Conservative Union, called me, and I volunteered to raise the $50,000 that Bill Brock and the Republican National Committee wouldn't give them.

Their call was one more proof of the reduced importance of political parties. And of the New Right's ability to engage in and finance important political activity outside a major political party.

I assured Laxalt and Crane that I could do the fundraising in two weeks time. But instead of raising $50,000, over $110,000 came in. I was assisted greatly on the mailing by Morton Blackwell, who also volunteered his time and expertise. We mailed two letters in one envelope—the first signed by Ronald Reagan and the second by Paul Laxalt. The extraordinary results confirmed that conservatives across the country felt as strongly about the Panama Canal as any issue in my lifetime.

Between the summer of 1977 and April 1978 when the final Senate votes occurred, the New Right sent between 7 and 9 million cards and letters to Americans asking them to: visit or write their Senators to express their views against the giveaway, write letters to newspaper editors, call in to TV and radio talk shows, ask organizations they belonged to to pass anti-Treaty resolutions, and send money so we could reach more Americans.

In all, the New Right spent about $3 million in an all-out effort to help save the Canal. We almost pulled it off.

The New Right fought Big Government, Big Business, Big Labor and Big Media to a standstill, for almost two years.

At the beginning of the battle, about 70% of the American people supported the New Right's position.

And after two years, we still had about 70% of the American people with us.

If I were the establishment, I would be worried. A handful of New Right conservatives almost beat them.

But mere numbers do not tell the whole story of the many individual sacrifices demanded and made.

Howard Phillips, the nearest thing to a perpetual motion machine that the New Right has, organized through The Conservative Caucus more than 12 major Keep-Our-Canal rallies, a nationwide billboard campaign, radio and TV spots, a phone bank, countless press conferences and speeches, and anti-Treaty campaigns in all 50 states.

Conservative Caucus field men slept in airports and bus stations while doing advance work for these events.

Terry Dolan and Paul Weyrich were unceasing in their lobbying efforts, urging their hundreds of thousands of supporters to contact their Senators and coaching their political candidates on how to make the most of the Canal issue.

Bill Rhatican, an expert publicist highly regarded for his sense of news and his ability to keep cool and good-humored in a crisis, skillfully guided the outside team's meetings.

John Laxalt, the Washington representative of Reagan's Citizens for the Republic, was of invaluable help to both the outside and inside teams.

On March 16, 1978, and again on April 18, 1978, we fell just two votes short. Needing 34 Senators to say "no," the Senate by a narrow margin of 68 to 32 voted to give away the Panama Canal.

But the New Right did not really lose. Our "defeat" became a victory seven months later when the American people went to the polls.

Our campaign to save the Canal gained conservative converts around the country—added more than 400,000 new names to our lists—encouraged many of the movement's leading figures (like Gordon Humphrey of New Hampshire) to run for public office—and produced significant liberal defeats in the fall.

In fact, since the Canal vote in 1978, 20 Senators who voted for the treaties have been defeated. Only one Senator who voted against the treaties (Robert Griffin of Michigan) was defeated.

The New Right came out of the Panama Canal fight with no casualties, not even a scar.

Because of Panama we are better organized. We developed a great deal of confidence in ourselves, and our opponents became weaker.

That November, the New Right really came of age.

For weeks, press speculation had mounted over the showing we would make. If we elected a good number of conservatives, we would be hailed as a major force in American politics. If not, liberals would begin writing our political obituary.

Frankly, the election returns exceeded even our most optimistic expectations. There were many victories we savored that night, but probably the two sweetest and unexpected by most political experts were those of Gordon Humphrey in New Hampshire and Roger Jepsen in Iowa.

Gordon Humphrey was the first U.S. Senator to come up through the ranks of the New Right. He was the newest of political newcomers, an Allegheny Airlines co-pilot until he announced for the Senate. At 37, Humphrey had never before run for public office, and had lived in New Hampshire only four years.

When Humphrey decided to run against veteran Democratic incumbent Tom McIntyre, he had little more than his personal life's savings to spend and the steadfast support of the many people he had met as New Hampshire state coordinator for The Conservative Caucus.

He was virtually unknown among the New Hampshire political establishment and given almost no chance to win.

But Humphrey proved his vote-getting ability, and surprised a lot of politicians, by receiving more votes in the GOP primary than his three opponents combined.

Humphrey campaigned across New Hampshire as a New Right conservative. "I want to be the toughest skinflint in the United States Senate," he said in his TV ads.

He was tough all the way—against gun control, against wasteful government spending. "I don't consider my role," he declared, "to see how much I can loot from the federal treasury."

Each senatorial candidate turned the election into a referendum.

Humphrey's referendum was McIntyre's vote to give away the Panama Canal and his overall liberal voting record.

McIntyre's referendum was the New Right. He attacked us on the floor of the U.S. Senate, on national television (via the "Today" show) and all across New Hampshire.

The people of New Hampshire backed Gordon Humphrey's referendum and rejected that of McIntyre, who after his defeat published a book attacking the New Right.

I must add here that Gordon might not have gotten across his New Right message and beaten his opponent without the superb assistance and, for a time, campaign management of Terry Dolan. When almost everyone else concluded McIntyre was unbeatable, Terry dug in harder, insisting Gordon Humphrey could win.

It was Terry Dolan who came up with the technique of aiming Boston TV at New Hampshire voters—an approach deemed by past campaign managers as too expensive and "wasteful" in its impact. But Terry had learned from campaign surveys and polls that thousands of new New Hampshire voters had recently moved from Massachusetts and were accustomed to watching Boston stations.

On election day, Gordon Humphrey pulled off the year's biggest political upset, defeating a 16-year incumbent senior senator 51—49%.

The political situation in Iowa was different. Republican Roger Jepsen was a former two-term lieutenant governor. For over a decade, he had been the state's leading conservative. He thought he had retired from politics (at a youthful 49), but decided to challenge Democratic Senator Dick Clark, feeling that the incumbent was just too liberal for Iowa.

In fact, the liberal Americans for Democratic Action identified Dick Clark as the most liberal member of the Senate. As chairman of the Africa subcommittee of the Senate Foreign Relations Committee, Clark was U.N. Ambassador Andrew Young's chief legislative supporter. The American Conservative Union gave Clark a conservative rating of 4%—worse than George McGovern's.

But in Iowa, Clark posed as a conservative, talking fiscal responsibility and limited government wherever he went.

So Jepsen hammered away at Clark for what he was —a big-spending liberal who voted one way in Washington and talked another way back home.

And the New Right turned out in force to help Jepsen. My company did the direct mail for him. Paul Weyrich's Committee for the Survival of a Free Congress and Terry Dolan's National Conservative Political Action Committee and Morton Blackwell's Committee for Responsible Youth Politics assisted him.

Right to Life groups heavily backed Jepsen, hitting hard at Clark's pro-abortion record.

The National Right to Work Committee did mailings and ran newspaper ads, comparing Clark's anti-Right to Work and Jepsen's pro-Right to Work stands—an important issue in a Right to Work state like Iowa.

Jepsen's aggressive hard-hitting campaign drove the truth home, and on November 7, 1978, he beat Dick Clark by 52% to 48%, adding another leaf to New Right laurels.

Other first-time winners for the New Right in the U.S. Senate were Bill Armstrong in Colorado, John Warner in Virginia and Alan Simpson in Wyoming. I must also mention one defeat—Jeff Bell in New Jersey.

Although Jeff lost to Democrat Bill Bradley in the general election, he beat aging veteran liberal Sen. Clifford Case in the Republican primary. Few thought Jeff had a chance, although *The New Right Report* flatly predicted in January that Case would be defeated in 1978. Jeff Bell told me that he could not have beaten Case and run as well as he did against Bradley without the enthusiastic nation-wide support of the New Right.

In the U.S. House of Representatives, conservatives also made sizeable gains. About 25 new GOP congressmen came from within the New Right ranks or became new supporters of the conservative movement.

And about 18 new Democratic conservatives won election. One of them, New Right Congressman Kent Hance of Texas, was elected president of the Democratic freshman class. They are Democrats who have good ties to the conservative movement, owe nothing to Big Labor bosses and largely avoided links with the Carter administration. Many of these Democrats received significant aid from New Right groups, usually in primaries.

Among these new Congressmen in both parties were Carroll Campbell from South Carolina, Bill Carney and Jerry Solomon from New York, Newt Gingrich of Georgia, Phil Gramm and Ron Paul from Texas, Jim

Jeffries from Kansas, Ken Kramer from Colorado and Bill Dannemeyer from California.

How did the New Right help swing these victories?

1. The most important single factor was the involvement of record numbers of new people on behalf of conservative candidates. Hundreds of thousands of people, for the first time in their lives, contributed to conservative candidates. Dedicated, concerned Americans who gave $1000, $100 or $10 made a big difference. These personal contributions were, by far, the largest source of funds for conservative candidates.

A handful of dedicated people like Weyrich, Dolan and others worked night and day to make this happen in 1978—in contrast with the unorganized efforts of conservatives a decade earlier.

2. The level of competence in conservative campaigns shot up dramatically. It was no accident. Dozens of conservative political action committees (PACs), conservative lobbying groups and educational organizations held approximately a hundred training schools and seminars on the political process and how to win elections in 1977-78. The schools were held all over the country, so a large pool of talented, trained conservatives was available almost everywhere.

Among the most active training programs were those sponsored by the Committee for the Survival of a Free Congress, the National Conservative Political Action Committee, Citizens for the Republic and the Committee for Responsible Youth Politics.

3. Conservative PACs made their campaign commitments carefully. When a race looked winnable, extra help and extra bucks were given.

New Right leaders made phone calls to corporate PACs telling them which campaigns were winnable. Direct mail, public relations and polling help were brought in for late and close elections.

National Stop-ERA, pro-gun, pro-life, Right to Work and other New Right leaders would contact their local members. Word was passed to ministers to get the message to their parishioners.

In contrast to previous years, very little conservative PAC help in 1978 went to unwinnable campaigns, no matter how "good" a conservative a candidate might have been.

For example, CSFC under Paul Weyrich spent $400,000 to help elect 31 conservative candidates—one of the best yields per dollar of any political group in the country.

Seventy percent of the candidates supported by Terry Dolan's NCPAC won, prompting the AFL-CIO's COPE to mourn:

"NCPAC . . . has created for the first time in our political history, an organization base for the Right that is in place and ready for action at a moment's notice in any campaign, at any level, anywhere in the country."

4. Conservative single-interest groups (pro-gun, pro-life, Right to Work, etc.) were effective. They attracted hundreds of thousands of previously uninvolved people into campaign activity. They made specially targeted mailings . . . held training schools . . . bought advertising exposing liberal voting records in their special interest publications . . . spent generously on purely lobbying and educational activities which raised public consciousness of their issues.

For example, after Mass on the Sunday before the November 7, 1978, election, most Iowa Catholics were handed a pamphlet contrasting Dick Clark's pro-abortion votes with Roger Jepsen's anti-abortion position.

In my opinion, the nation owes a major debt to single-purpose groups in the areas of Right to Work, Right to Life, tax limitation, defense and pro-gun activity.

5. More than in past years, growing numbers of business and association PACs spent their money wisely on free enterprise and national defense candidates. But many business PACs still showered their money on liberal incumbents and even liberal challengers.

However, one of the major accomplishments of the New Right has been to swing corporate and association PACs from heavily supporting liberals toward a much greater role in helping conservatives.

The following analysis by *The New Right Report* shows a significant shift by four such PACs between 1976 and 1978. It shows what percentage of their money the PACs of these groups gave to liberals in contested races for the U.S. House and Senate.

	1976	1978
Chicago & Northwestern Transportation Company	92.9% liberal	27% liberal
National Forest Products Association	100.0% liberal	39% liberal
Weyerhaeuser Corporation	61.9% liberal	17% liberal
Georgia Pacific	44.8% liberal	16% liberal

In 1980, the support of conservative rather than liberal candidates by corporate and association PACs appears to have been even greater.

6. Conservative activity was not limited to GOP candidates. Involvement in Democratic politics by conservative activists was a major development for the conservative cause in 1978.

In some cases, conservative Democrats had little or no GOP opposition. In other cases, supposedly unbeatable liberal Democrats were upset by conservative Democrats running conservative campaigns (backed by the New Right) in the primary.

In 1978, the New Right discovered that there is more than one way to skin a liberal in a campaign.

There was the Jesse Helms example. By his devoted efforts on behalf of almost every conservative cause during his first term, Senator Helms of North Carolina became a hero of the conservative movement. In his 1978 reelection campaign, a strong direct mail effort attracted about $7 million from 190,000 contributors, including 30,000 in North Carolina. These mailings, begun two years before his reelection, enabled the Helms campaign to organize at every level for an almost unprecedented grassroots effort.

There was the Mickey Edwards example. Before his 2,644 vote victory in 1976, Congressman Edwards of Oklahoma and his wife Sue personally knocked on more than 40,000 doors in his district. Such personal contact builds lasting ties. In Congress, Mickey paid a lot of personal attention to all voters in his district, especially black voters.

He convinced them that conservative ideas are the best ideas in the long run for all Americans. He showed, for example, how the liberal-imposed minimum wage increases unemployment among young blacks. As a result, Mickey Edwards won reelection in 1978 with 80% of the vote, including 75% of both black and labor voters.

There was the Bob Kasten example. Robert Kasten of Wisconsin developed a volunteer recruitment plan which enabled him, in his U.S. House races, to enlist a large number of enthusiastic workers. These volunteers then organized an intensive voter identification drive, finding and persuading enough voters to elect Kasten repeatedly to Congress. In 1980 he was elected to the Senate.

In 1976, 1978 and 1980, largely through the Committee for the Survival of a Free Congress, many conservative candidates used the Kasten plan to win nominations and elections. For example, Bruce Erickson, campaign manager for Republican Jim Jeffries, who upset liberal Congresswoman Martha Keys (D—Kan.), says flatly: "It was the (Kasten plan) organization which pulled us through."

Ironically, Bob neglected to use his own plan in the GOP primary when he ran for governor of Wisconsin in 1978. As a result, he lost the GOP primary because he was waiting for the November general election before starting the Kasten plan. You can be certain he used it in his successful 1980 Senate race.

These techniques were used by the New Right in 1978 and 1980 to become a major force in American politics.

We won far more than a number of important races in the U.S. Senate and House of Representatives. We helped shift the entire spectrum of politics to the right.

I doubt that a dozen liberal candidates for Congress, if they were strongly challenged, admitted they were liberals.

Incumbents with the most left-wing records proclaimed they were against deficits, red tape and interfering bureaucrats. Veteran liberals suddenly sang the praises of free enterprise and a strong national defense. They knew they had to, or go down to certain defeat.

The conservative momentum achieved in 1978 has not subsided but has increased.

Conservatives will dominate the 1980s, I predict, because most of our leaders are now coming into their own, while most of the liberal leaders are dead, retired or just too tired to compete in the demanding decade before us.

VIII

The Four Keys
to Our Success

Our success is built on four elements — single issue groups, multi-issue conservative groups, coalition politics and direct mail.

Conservative single issue groups have been accused of not only fragmenting American politics but threatening the very existence of our two-party system. Congressman David Obey of Wisconsin, a liberal Democrat, has even charged that government has nearly been brought to a standstill by single issue organizations.

Nonsense!

In the first place, all the New Right has done is copy the success of the old left.

Liberal single issue groups were around long before we were, and the liberals still have as many or more than we do.

Civil rights was a single issue that Hubert Humphrey used to rise to national office. The Vietnam War was a single issue that George McGovern used to rise to national prominence. The environment, consumerism, anti-nuclear power — these are all single issues around which liberals have organized and exercised power and influence.

In the area of public interest law, liberal groups such as the Environmental Defense Fund, the National Prison

Project, the Mexican-American Legal Defense and Education Fund, the Southern Poverty Law Center, the National Veterans Law Center, the Women's Legal Defense Fund have drastically changed the direction of the federal government.

Ralph Nader is nothing if not a collection of single issues. The liberals who are upset now about conservative single issue groups were not upset about the groups pushing for legalization of marijuana. . .homosexual rights . . . or ERA.

As columnist John Roche, a former chairman of the liberal Americans for Democratic Action, wrote in June 1980 about single issue groups:

"The conservatives learned to play from us. The labor movement, for example, employed one-issue politics with spectacular success for years. Like my grandpa, they would have supported a baboon if it endorsed increasing the minimum wage."

And as columnists Jack Germond and Jules Witcover wrote in the *Washington Star*:

"By taking such an approach, the conservatives are essentially following the same strategy that made the liberal coalition in the Democratic Party the dominant force in our politics over the last several decades."

And as columnist John Chamberlain wrote: "The technique of coalition building is open to anybody. It is as old as American politics. . . Let's have no tears about it — it will continue to be the way in America as long as the republic stands."

Here are just some of the better known liberal single issue groups:

- Sierra Club
- National Organization of Women (NOW)
- Congressional Black Caucus
- Planned Parenthood
- SANE
- Gay Rights National Lobby
- National Abortion Rights Action League
- Public Citizen (Ralph Nader's key organization)
- Wilderness Society
- Women Strike for Peace

Could it be the real reason why they're upset is that conservative single issue groups are becoming more and more effective and having more and more impact on the political process, as in the 1978 defeat of liberals Dick Clark, Tom McIntyre and others?

In 1980 Senator George McGovern said he failed to understand voters who would look at only one issue in a Senator's record while ignoring all the other issues. That's because McGovern was worried about reelection in 1980 and right to life forces were a large part of his worry. "But McGovern was singing quite another tune," Paul Weyrich reminds us, "when he encouraged leftist groups to make the war *the* issue that counted 10 years ago."

And there is far less liberal legislation being passed in the Congress as a result of conservative single issue groups. Liberal proposals like labor law "reform," consumer protection, common situs picketing, changes in the Hatch Act, instant voter registration and taxpayer financing of Congressional elections were stopped dead by conservative opposition.

Second, single issue groups naturally emerge because the political parties run away from the issues. Single issue groups are the result not the cause of the decline of political parties.

If one of the two major political parties had concerned itself more with issues like right to life, high taxes, the growth of the federal government, the right to keep and bear arms, a strong national defense, prayer in the schools, strengthening the family, sex on TV and in the movies, there probably would not have been an explosion of conservative single issue groups.

For example, about 70% of the American public opposed giving our Panama Canal to a Marxist dictator. And probably about 85% of Republicans opposed the giveaway.

What was the official and unofficial position of the Republican National Committee? They wanted nothing to do with the issue.

But, the RNC didn't mind at all raising more than $700,000 from conservative Republicans by sending out fund raising letters asking for money to help defeat the Panama Canal treaties.

But when Ronald Reagan and Paul Laxalt went to the chairman of the Republican National Committee in December 1977 to ask for $50,000 to fight the Panama Canal giveaway, they were told that the Republican party was going to stay away from this controversial issue. (See Chapter 7.)

And in 1978 we saw Senator Robert Packwood, chairman of the Senate Republican Campaign Committee, supervising the raising of large sums of money from conservative Republicans (again via direct mail) on the single issue of labor law reform and the general subject of abuses of power by Washington union officials.

But how did Senator Packwood vote on the legislation? You guessed it. He voted for labor law reform and against the position of his Committee's fund raising letters. By the way, in 1980, he received over $32,000 from unions for his 1980 reelection to the Senate.

So as the Republican and Democratic parties avoided taking stands on controversial issues, citizens interested in those issues, out of their frustration and concern, banded together to make sure their views were represented.

Political parties have no one to blame but themselves for the breakdown and possible breakup of political parties.

Furthermore, both parties supported a law which made special interest groups all the more inevitable—the Federal Election Campaign Act of 1974. The act's intent was to get so-called "special interests" out of politics. But the result has been that single issue groups are into politics as they never were before the 1974 elections.

They have been significantly helped by the $1000 ceiling placed on the amount of money an individual may give to a candidate or committee. The new restriction forced candidates to find ways to finance elections outside the normal two-party structure.

Single issue groups sprang up and plunged into politics, writing letters, forming PACs, getting involved in campaigns. Millions of letters were written. Tens of millions of dollars were raised. Thousands of activists entered the political process.

Some candidates, instead of depending upon handouts from their national parties, put together their own large list of financial supporters, almost always through direct mail. Senator Jesse Helms showed how it could be done in his 1978 campaign when more than 190,000 people contributed nearly $7 million to his reelection. Those 190,000 contributors today give Jesse a financial and political base unsurpassed by any other Senator in American history. Consequently, the national Republican Party has next to no ability to influence Helms.

And thanks to the liberals and the national media who insisted on the passage of the 1974 election law, many Congressmen and Senators have 20,000, 30,000, 40,000 and some 50,000 and more individual contributors averaging $15 to $20 per contribution. As a result, the day of the traditional political boss issuing orders to Congressmen is gone in most parts of America.

The Jesse Helms' operation in Raliegh, North Carolina has to be seen to be believed. Called the Congressional Club, it has seven departments, ranging from administration to advertising, a permanent staff of 40 (150 in an election year) and an annual budget that exceeded $6 million in 1980.

The Club's honorary chairman and guiding spirit is Senator Helms. The chairman is Tom Ellis and the treasurer is Carter Wrenn—two of the most effective New Right leaders in America.

In 1980 the Congressional Club helped 51 congressional and senatorial candidates as well as 20 state legislative candidates. It also spent $4.7 million in an independent campaign for Ronald Reagan.

It has its own computer operation, its own mailing operation and its own printing shop. The Club provided the key organizers who led the 1980 upset victory of New Right Senator John East over incumbent Robert Morgan.

A sister operation is the Coalition for Freedom, an educational foundation, which distributes such films as "The Shining City on a Hill," featuring Senator Helms and Ronald Reagan.

I believe we need *more* not fewer single issue groups. As Senator Jake Garn of Utah put it at a New Right meeting in early 1979: "Political parties react to public pressure. Ten years ago, even five years ago, virtually all the public pressure was generated by the Left. Today we're catching up, but we have a long way to go. We need more new and more effective groups.

Yes, we need ethnic groups. . . elderly groups. . . black middle class groups. . . blue collar groups. . . anti-busing groups. . . welfare reform groups. We need a group for every important issue in America so that the rights of the conservative majority in America will be adequately represented.

However, these groups would not be as necessary and certainly would not be as powerful as they are today if the Republican or Democratic party would effectively take up these single issues.

The second key to our success is the multi-issue group which is part of the conservative movement and makes no bones about it. Such a group is conservative first, last and always. It takes strong positions on every important conservative vs. liberal issue.

The multi-issue conservative movement group also takes a broad over-view of where we are going and the best way to get there.

It usually does not have as many members or supporters as single issue groups because its ranks are made up of individuals who are solidly conservative across the board.

The National Right to Work Committee can find over a million people who strongly oppose compulsory unionism.

The National Rifle Association can find nearly two million people who support opposition to federal gun registration.

Right to Life groups can find over a million people who oppose abortion.

But a conservative group which is pro-Right to Work, pro-Right to Life and pro-gun simply can't find a million contributors who agree on 20 different conservative issues.

For example, a local union leader may dislike the National Right to Work Committee but also oppose additional gun controls.

A pro-life supporter may not care one way or the other about compulsory unionism. And so forth.

But it is a sign of conservative strength that several of our broad spectrum groups do have, if not a million members, several hundred thousand.

Multi-issue broad spectrum groups such as The Conservative Caucus, the American Conservative Union, the Committee for the Survival of a Free Congress, the Heritage Foundation and the National Conservative Political Action Committee, to name but a few, are trying and succeeding in covering all the bases and all the issues for the conservative movement.

These movement groups are led by generalists like Paul Weyrich and Howard Phillips, who have well thought out positions on almost every issue. These groups are sensitive to all the elements of the growing conservative coalition. Their leaders can talk the language of all the single issue groups so vital to conservative growth.

When a Right to Work expert lectures at a Right to Life workshop on lobbying, it's a safe bet that a conservative movement leader had a hand in planning the workshop.

It is these leaders who work night and day to expand the leadership, educate each other in winning techniques and build ever larger and more influential coalitions.

I want to say something here about the internal dynamics of how we do things.

Some people think we are a big conspiracy. Others think we meet and vote on everything we do. Others think I give orders to everyone. These are all false ideas.

I have helped start a number of New Right groups, but I don't "control" any of them.

When we get together, we never vote on anything. Usually someone leads the discussion, but he has no more authority than anyone else present.

We exchange information. We brainstorm new ideas. Some people volunteer to do something or commit their organizations to do specific things. But no one gives orders like a commander-in-chief, or a Godfather.

Some gatherings are weekly, some twice a month, some annually, and so forth. But the majority are ad hoc.

We meet to work on special projects, say a piece of legislation. We meet as often as is necessary to do the best job we can for the conservative side of the issue.

We often bring in different leaders for different kinds of issues. We are creative in convincing different groups that their interests are the same as ours in particular battles.

That's how we got a broad spectrum of allies to fight instant voter registration, taxpayer campaign financing and other liberal election law power grabs.

Our informal way of operating is very frustrating to liberals who would love to have us tied up in formal organizations which would be easier to attack. But how do you use guilt by association against informal, ad hoc discussion groups?

Which brings me to the third part of the New Right's success — coalition politics.

Coalition politics is as old as the United States of America. You could call the original Thirteen Colonies a collection of issue groups who banded together to fight and defeat a common enemy — Great Britain.

The Republican Party was originally a coalition of issue groups — Free-Soil party members, pro-business northern Whigs, and some Democrats opposed to slavery.

FDR's New Deal was basically a coalition of groups — Southern farmers, blacks, Jews, organized labor, big city Democrats and the unemployed.

In fact, a liberal coalition based on the New Deal, the Fair Deal and the Great Society has dominated the nation for almost five decades.

But in the last 12 years, since Hubert Humphrey lost the Presidency to Richard Nixon in 1968, that coalition has begun to unravel. Conservatives didn't have the institutions to fill the gap then, but we do now.

Senator James McClure of Idaho has pointed out that conservative coalitions are forming in several different ways:

1. Outright Democrat-Republican coalitions in legislative leadership elections such as that of Robert Monier as president of the New Hampshire Senate. Monier proclaims: "We no longer have a minority party and a majority party. We have a majority coalition and a minority coalition."

2. Special group coalitions in elections such as the victories of Roger Jepsen in Iowa and Gordon Humphrey in New Hampshire, 1978, where supporters of Right to Life and Right to Work, gun owners, taxpayers, those favoring a strong national defense and others came together. These coalitions were also extremely active in 1980, especially in the victories of Steve Symms in Idaho, Chuck Grassley in Iowa, Al D'Amato in New York and Don Nickles in Oklahoma.

Such coalitions have also upset liberals in local races, like Helen Wise, former national chairman of the National Education Association union.

Mrs. Wise was elected a Pennsylvania state representative in 1976 with 62% of the vote. In 1978, despite the fact that her district includes the huge student population of Penn State University, Mrs. Wise was defeated by a young conservative attorney, Greg Cunningham, 51-49%.

At a subsequent Washington, D.C. meeting on the "threat" of the New Right, Mrs. Wise described herself as a "victim of some kind of right coalition." Because conservatives are coalescing, she said, there "aren't any more pure, single issues. And that's our problem." She listed the following issues as contributing to her defeat:

Taxes. Pennsylvania is a hyper-tax state, she said. She was astounded that her vote for "a tax which put 150 million dollars into the public schools of Pennsylvania" could be used against her in her university-dominated district.

Abortion. "It's going to be a force and you can't treat it in isolation," she warned, referring to the pro-life movement. Even in her "very liberal district," her pro-abortion votes generated fierce opposition. Wise reported that in her district, the most visible anti-abortionists "were not Catholics, they were fundamental religious groups."

Gun control. "I've never really taken a position" on the issue, Wise said. But she voted twice for the constitutional amendment which would almost certainly give D.C. two anti-gun liberal Democratic U.S. Senators and that, she said, cemented a coalition of sportsmen and rural Republicans which opposed her.

Right to Work. "An innocuous little bill which I voted for," she said, which would give some "meet and confer" powers sought by teachers' unions, made her a target of foes of compulsory unionism. Wise said that "more Right to Work material came out in our state in the last two years than ever before in its history."

Equal Rights Amendment. ERA, she said, "has not been an issue in Pennsylvania in seven or eight years." But she introduced a package of 26 bills to implement the state ERA. Then "all those who were vocally opposed to any kind of abortion or abortion choice, they suddenly also latched on the anti-ERAs, so they brought a few more people in."

Despite her analysis, Mrs. Wise revealed she didn't understand the conservative movement when she complained, "I was never accused of being immoral, just a lack of moral leadership, whatever that is."

In New York, the new Right-to-Life Party, led by Mary Jane Tobin, drew 130,000 votes in the November 1978 gubernatorial election, assuring itself the fourth place on the ballot for the next four years. In fifth place is the Liberal Party.

"It is essential," says Senator McClure, "that conservatives provide the leadership for those disaffected from the power structure or someone else will."

Coalition politics was being considered in the early 1970s by the Nixon White House. It was aimed at persuading Southern Democrats to change parties and thus take over the U.S. House of Representatives. But then Watergate came along, and coalitions fell victim to Nixon's problems as did a lot of other plans.

In the 1980s, the New Right is determined to do away with old-style politics.

In the past, liberals practiced coalition politics successfully while conservatives limited themselves to the Republican Party. No wonder we were such a small minority.

To put it bluntly, we were snookered. The liberals said what is ours is ours — the Democratic Party — and what is yours — the Republican Party — is negotiable.

So the liberals for many years have had almost 100% of the national Democratic Party and about 40% of the national Republican Party — giving the liberals about 70% of the political elections.

How can conservatives ever expect to govern if we concede 100% of the larger of the two major parties to the liberals without any fight and limit our fight to the political party which represents about 20% of the voters?

But the New Right is not willing to play by the liberals' rules. We are more than willing to support Democrats as long as they are Democrats who are basically right of center. It's a matter of simple arithmetic and common sense.

I want to make it clear that coalition politics does not necessarily mean a third party.

The impulse of some conservatives after Watergate (myself included) was to try to organize a brand new broadly based party, designed to replace the Republican Party. But the two-party system was, and is, probably too solidly entrenched for any such effort. It is a fact of life that Democratic and Republican politicians have written national and state laws in such a way that it's almost impossible to start a new political party.

Coalition politics includes working within the Republican and Democratic parties to nominate conservative candidates, promote conservative positions and create conservative majorities in both parties.

We must always be firm in putting principle before party. Some New Right leaders are established activists who fight for conservative principles within the Republican or Democratic parties. I used to think of myself as a Republican. Now I'm an Independent. And I have plenty of company. About 38% of the American electorate describe themselves as Independent.

Conservatives have the strength, the resources and the ability to operate in both major parties. In fact, because the Democratic Party is so much larger, there are many more conservative Democrats than conservative Republicans when you add up all the blue collar, ethnic, Catholic and other social conservative Democrats.

To sum it up, conservatives should neither abandon the Republicans nor ignore the Democrats.

We do not seek to eliminate the present political structures but to influence them to adopt the conservative point of view which we believe to be that of the majority of the American people.

Let me give you an example of the difference one conservative can make.

In February 1977, I wrote an article in *Conservative Digest* urging conservatives to get more active in the Democratic Party. Bob Perry, a Houston, Texas, home builder, read my column and persuaded a conservative Democrat to run against Congressman Bob Gammage in the Democratic primary. The conservative Democrat got almost 44% of the vote and successfully identified Gammage (who spent about $100,000 in the primary) as a liberal in the minds of the voters.

In the fall, Republican Ron Paul, who had won and lost close contests against Gammage in previous Congressional elections, beat Gammage by about 2,000 votes. Without that conservative challenge in the Democratic primary (which cost Gammage both time and money that he couldn't spend against Ron Paul), Gammage would almost certainly have won.

In truth, the political parties have been so weakened that in many areas they are like big battleships without rudders or ammunition. The time has come for conservatives to make the effort needed to influence and, where possible, provide direction for these powerful political institutions.

Each party is a goldmine of opportunity. Each has local, state and national committees, Congressional campaign committees and Senatorial campaign committees as well as women's groups, college groups and teenage groups. These committees have important legal powers, huge spending capabilities, easy access to news media coverage and are often the key role in picking who will be the party nominee.

And that is all important. As Tammany Hall leaders said in the 19th century: Let us pick the nominees. Then the people can elect whoever they want in November.

Conservatives should work for the day when the November election is between a conservative Democrat and a conservative Republican. Then we can go fishing or play golf on election day knowing that it doesn't matter if a Republican or Democrat wins — it's only important that a conservative wins.

Probably about 90% of the November elections for the past 30 years have been between a liberal Democrat and a liberal Republican or a liberal Democrat and a conservative Republican. And since only about 20% of the voters consider themselves Republicans, how can conservatives, if they work only in the Republican Party, come to power in the next five to ten years at the city, county, state and national level?

Occasionally, if the Democrats make enough mistakes and Republicans offer a strong candidate, we can win a Presidential race. But that's not governing America. Conservatives may control the U.S. Senate now, but liberal Democrats and liberal Republicans will still control a majority in the U.S. House of Representatives, of the governors, of state legislatures, of the mayors, of county officials, etc.

State laws and party customs vary, but here are some of the specific powers of political party committees, as outlined by New Right analyst Morton Blackwell:

Elect party officers. . . control raising and spending of party funds. . . set dates, sites, rules and fees of party conventions which nominate or endorse candidates for public office. . . name new nominees when candidates die or withdraw before a general election. . . establish candidate recruitment procedures. . . control or strongly influence the election process of each state's delegates to national party conventions and members of national committees. . . pass resolutions on controversial public issues. . . endorse or condemn any public officeholder . . . provide valuable public forums for selected leaders or political candidates.

All of these powers can be summed up in one sentence: most of the political power in the United States is channeled through political party structures.

Right now, as you are reading this, there probably are vacancies on the party committees in the town or county where you live. Often you can get a seat immediately on a local party committee just by expressing your interest to the local party chairman. In other cases, you might have to wait a year or so before a new committee is elected in a primary or at a local party meeting.

Every political party has a crying need for volunteers. You will find that working a bit in your spare time on party projects will give you a leg up on most of the others who might want to serve on party committees.

There is a rapid turnover in most party leadership positions, which means a determined person can rise in the ranks very quickly. Liberals (and politicians with no philosophy) usually control party groups only by default. So very few people take part in party organizations that even a little input of conservative energy will work big changes quickly.

I want to talk now about the fourth reason for the New Right's success — direct mail.

Like all successful political movements, we must have a method of communicating with each other, and for conservatives in the 1970s, it was direct mail.

Frankly, the conservative movement is where it is today because of direct mail. Without direct mail, there would be no effective counterforce to liberalism, and certainly there would be no New Right.

Some of the most common complaints I hear from conservatives are:

"I get too much mail." "I received six letters from one organization this month." "I get letters from twenty groups." "Why don't conservatives get together and form one organization?"

You may not have thought of it, but the U.S. mail is the principle method of communication for conservatives.

We sell our magazines, our books, and our candidates through the mail. We fight our legislative battles through the mail. We alert our supporters to upcoming battles through the mail. We find new recruits for the conservative movement through the mail.

Without the mail, most conservative activities would wither and die.

Most political observers agree that liberals have effective control of the mass media — a virtual monopoly on TV, radio, newspapers and magazines.

Walter Cronkite of CBS, Katherine Graham, head of the *Washington Post* and *Newsweek*, the heads of the *New York Times*, NBC, ABC, *Time* — to paraphrase Patrick Buchanan — draw up the agenda for the nation's public business. They determine who shall be heard and seen, what subjects shall be discussed, and for how long.

They decide that it's cost overruns in the military that is a major story and not cost overruns in the Welfare Department.

It's not that the media presents the news in a partisan way, it's that they present the positive side of liberal causes, liberal issues, liberal personalities and, for the most part, ignore conservative causes, conservative issues and conservative personalities or present them in an unfavorable manner.

However, there is one method of mass commercial communication that the liberals do not control — direct mail. In fact, conservatives excel at direct mail.

There's an old saying that if a tree fell in a forest and no one was in the forest, it didn't make any noise.

Well, before conservatives started using direct mail in a major way, many of our good candidates, books, magazines, ideas, causes were unknown and ineffective because there was no method to tell the public about them — no one heard them.

Without direct mail, for example, President Ford would almost certainly have signed the common situs bill in January, 1976. But in the fall of 1975, the National Right to Work Committee mailed over 4 million letters to people likely to agree with them on this issue. The mailings resulted in 720,000 letters and post-cards to the White House, urging a presidential veto.

But without direct mail advertising, most conservatives would not have known that Ford was about to sign the bill. And even if they had heard about it, most would not have known what action to take.

The letters from the Right to Work Committee explained the issue, explained how pressure could be put on the President to veto common situs, included a postcard addressed to Ford, and asked for a contribution to help pay for the cost of the direct mail advertising campaign.

Ford caved in and vetoed common situs which he had promised his secretary of labor, and then AFL-CIO head George Meany, he would sign.

This same approach has been used many times by conservatives to help beat the Consumer Protection Agency, labor law reform, federal financing of Congressional elections, unionization of the military, SALT II, changes in the Hatch Act, etc., etc.

Congressmen Philip and Dan Crane of Illinois, George Hansen of Idaho, Robert Dornan of California, Bob Livingston of Louisiana, Mickey Edwards of Oklahoma and many other conservatives probably wouldn't be in Congress now if it weren't for national direct mail appeals for their campaigns.

In May 1980, I attended the dedication of the Joseph and Holly Coors and Edward Noble Buildings of the Heritage Foundation in Washington, D.C. Each building was made possible by a very generous contribution of these three people—and by direct mail.

Without direct mail, we might have no *National Review*, no *Human Events*, no *Conservative Digest*, no conservative PACs, no effective organizations in Right to Work, Right to Life, pro-gun, anti-busing, national defense, pro-family, no large national conservative organizations and youth training.

You can think of direct mail as *our* TV, radio, daily newspaper and weekly magazine.

Some people persist in thinking of direct mail as only fund raising. But it's really mostly advertising.

Raising money is only one of several purposes of direct-mail advertising letters. A letter may ask you to vote for a candidate, volunteer for campaingn work, circulate a petition among your neighbors, write letters and postcards to your Senators and Congressmen, urging them to pass or defeat legislation and also ask you for money to pay for the direct mail advertising campaign.

Direct mail is, in fact, the third largest form of advertising in the country, spending about $7.3 billion in 1978, third only to television and newspapers.

"Junk mail," by the way, is a phrase probably first used by the Scripps-Howard newspapers in the 1940s. I can understand why they did it. After all, direct mail was then the number one competitior of newspapers for the advertising dollar.

It is a unique form of advertising. If done properly, it pays for itself which is something almost no other form of advertising can do for conservatives.

It is the advertising medium of the underdog. It allows organizations or causes not part of the mainstream to get funding.

Direct mail is the advertising medium of the non-establishment candidate.

Sometimes the giants of TV and radio make decisions, for whatever reason, that stifle free speech.

For example, the three major TV networks, ABC, NBC and CBS, established a policy of not selling time to any political candidate in 1979.

That decision may not hurt you if you are the President of the U.S. with all of the power that goes with the office. But if you are Senator Kennedy, it can keep your campaign from getting off to a proper start.

And again, the networks' decision may not be a serious problem if you are the front runner in the G.O.P. with 35% support, as Ronald Reagan was in the summer of 1979. But it can be a devastating blow if you are John Connally with 10% support and want to get on TV to promote your candidacy.

The three major networks seriously damaged John Connally's ability to win the Republican nomination by keeping him off TV in 1979.

George McGovern became the Democratic presidential nominee in 1972 because of direct mail.

Through direct mail, McGovern found about 250,000 supporters who financed his race. From this list of 250,000, McGovern's field organizers were given the names of individuals which were used in organizing for primaries and caucuses.

When he couldn't afford to advertise on television, McGovern could spend $200,000 (mostly on credit) to write to 1 million identified liberal Democrats, knowing that an appeal for money in the letters would bring in enough funds within 30 days to pay for the direct mail advertising.

So George McGovern and his brilliant direct mail team of Morris Dees and Tom Collins used the mails to bypass the party bosses, the party establishment, and the smoke-filled rooms to go straight to the people.

Most of the news media didn't understand political direct mail, until George McGovern came along that year and made it an acceptable political tool.

Independent presidential candidate John Anderson depended heavily on direct mail. In the first part of 1980, his direct mail expert Roger Craver was mailing to his house file (those who had already given to Anderson) about once every eight days.

In fact, I feel confident that John Anderson would not have been a serious candidate for President in 1980 without David Garth and Roger Craver. While most politically knowledgeable people have heard of Garth, an outstanding TV and political expert, very few have heard of Craver.

But without Craver, John Anderson would not have had the money to travel around the country (and to Europe and the Middle East in July) and buy TV and radio ads. He would have been just another minor candidate who never caught fire.

In 1980, Craver mailed 10 million letters, developed a list of 240,000 contributors, and raised $16.5 million through direct mail for John Anderson.

George McGovern, John Anderson, Jesse Helms — they all understand that direct mail is basically an advertising medium. And they understand that repetition is absolutely necessary.

If you see three ads for Coca Cola in one day, you don't get upset or think the Coke people are wasting their money. If you are a Ford Motor Co. stockholder and you see five ads for Ford cars in one week, you don't get upset and think that they are wasting your money. It's the same way with direct mail.

By the way, to the best of my knowledge, in no other country do people give money to political causes through the mails as we do in America.

Look at what happened to Congressman Phil Crane. He took a $15,000 investment in the summer of 1978 and by using direct mail became an active and serious candidate.

With that $15,000 (a personal loan to his presidential committee), he was able to raise more than $5 million (including about $2 million matching money from the government) with which he promoted conservative ideas, compiled a list of 80,000 contributors, and aimed his candidacy for President at those Republicans likely to vote in GOP primaries.

Direct mail was the only advertising medium that made sense for Phil Crane.

I want to say just a few words about the cost of direct mail. First of all, the organization that profits the most from mailing is the U.S. Post Office. Out of every dollar spent on direct mail, about 35 to 40 cents goes for postage.

Then there are the costs of printing the letter, the brochure and other enclosures, plus the envelopes. You also have to pay the mailing house, mailing list owner, and the advertising agency which creates and coordinates the entire package.

It is not a cheap medium, but it is a highly effective one if you know what you're doing. And conservatives do. That's why liberals are always screaming about direct mail and trying to figure out ways — like cutting the amount of money PACs can give to a candidate, preventing Congressmen and Senators from using exact reproductions of their official stationery for letters helping non-profit organziations, and public financing of Congressional campaigns — to make direct mail less effective for us.

Where would conservatives be without direct mail? We would be where we were 20 years ago, on the defensive, isolated, fighting losing battles.

Some years back, a few of my fellow conservatives were critical of me. They said I was mailing too much and that I should not help new organizations get started. They took the approach that the conservative resources were like a pie to be divided among several organizations. They were worried about more groups cutting it into thinner and thinner slices. They feared that their own organizations would get smaller slices of the conservative money pie.

I rejected that philosophy. I felt that if we only had about 100,000 potential conservative contributors in the nation, we were wasting our time trying to beat the liberals. I knew you couldn't turn the country around with only 100,000 contributors.

I felt there were millions of Americans who would contribute if asked. So I and others set out to find and identify millions of new conservative contributors and supporters. We found them, I'm happy to say. The Viguerie Co. now has some 4½ million people we can identify as having indicated an interest in a conservative candidate or cause over the last four years. I think we can add at least another 5 million in the next three years.

Most of these new 5 million conservative contributions will come from the conservative Christian community. They will contribute because they want to stop abortions, do away with sex and violence on TV, bring voluntary prayer back to school, stop busing, etc.

There is another key to New Right success — our positive attitude toward the news media.

From the time I started in politics in the mid 1950s until the mid 1970s, most conservatives and the national media were like cats and dogs, or oil and water — they just didn't mix.

Then in the mid 1970s, some of the national media began to notice our political activities.

I have to be honest and say that I shared the traditional conservatives' position on the press. Which was avoid them, recognize that they are all liberals, and be convinced that their basic purpose is to attack conservatives.

I remember one day a fairly well known writer for a major newspaper called and wanted an appointment to come and talk to me.

I was a little short of terrified. I told my secretary to tell him I'd get back to him.

I then called some of my conservative associates and asked what I should do. Almost all advised me to avoid the reporter.

The advice went something like this — that newspaper is no friend of the conservative movement, that reporter will try to do you in, etc., etc.

But then I got to thinking. I and my conservative friends are not playing in the big leagues — but we want to.

We're not having a major influence on national policies — but we want to.

We're not close to our goal of governing America— but we want to.

I called the reporter back and said, "Why don't you come over and, if you've got time, why don't we have lunch?"

Well, I spent an enjoyable three hours with the reporter. He wrote a basically fair and accurate story (although it wasn't as fair and objective as my mother would have written).

And from that day forward, I felt that I and other conservatives had to change our view of the press.

I can think of no better example of the difference between the New Right and the old right.

We realize that reporters and editors are not monsters, or even hopeless ideologues.

The vast majority are good, decent men and women who are trying to do a professional job and are looking for the kind of news which will put their stories on the front page or the nightly TV newscasts.

During the next few years, the New Right's relationship with the press improved. We felt comfortable with the press and they began to cover our activities.

However, in the spring of 1977 I realized that my associates in the New Right and I needed a more professional approach to the media.

We were dealing with the media in a casual, almost accidental way. We needed someone to introduce us to the major media, to teach us how to call and conduct a press conference, how to have a press breakfast, how to get our thoughts across in a few seconds on TV, how to hold activities that the press would be interested in covering.

So in April 1977, Bill Rhatican came into the New Right's life.

Bill had been press secretary to Treasury Secretary Bill Simon and Interior Secretary Rogers Morton and a top aid to Ron Nessen in the Ford White House.

I hired Bill to be vice president of public affairs at The Viguerie Co. He immediately threw himself heavily into key battles then being waged by the New Right — the Panama Canal, instant voter registration and taxpayer financing of Congressional Elections.

And another big step forward was taken by the New Right.

Single issue groups — multi-issue groups — coalition politics — direct mail — these have been the four cornerstones of conservative growth and success in the 1970's. They will help us build a new majority in America in the 1980's.

As Congressman Newt Gingrich of Georgia has put it: "The way you build a majority in this country is you go out and put together everybody who's against the guy who's in. And instead of asking the question, What divides us?, you ask the question, What unites us?"

And what unites most conservatives, Republican, Democratic and Independent, is a desire for less government and more freedom for every American.

IX

The New Leaders

So far I have discussed the New Right in a general way. Perhaps this is the moment to speak more specifically about some of our leaders. Because the New Right is such a dynamic phenomenon, it would be impossible to list them all, let alone put them in any order of importance. After all, the New Right is a loose federation of people with common purposes—not a hierarchy under centralized control.

Paul Weyrich, Howard Phillips, Terry Dolan, Morton Blackwell are four young men who have played an important role in the spectacular development of the New Right. But there are others who more than deserve mention for their significant contributions over the years:

• Alan Gottlieb is executive director of the Citizens Committee for the Right to Keep and Bear Arms. Gottlieb's Second Amendment Foundation is a highly effective legal aid group working to stop the liberals' drive to disarm U.S. citizens. A whole cluster of effective New Right groups are rising from Alan's modern facility in Bellevue, Washington.

• Lt. Gen. Daniel Graham (USA-ret.) is the New Right's top security expert and spokesman. As co-chairman of the Coalition for Peace Through Strength, Dan Graham (a former director of the Defense Intelligence Agency) was one of the three or four most important leaders in our thus-far successful fight against Senate ratification of SALT II. He was also in the forefront of the conservative battles against the Panama Canal treaties and the nomination of Paul Warnke to be director of the Arms Control and Disarmament Agency.

• Reed Larson is president of the National Right to Work Committee, which spearheaded the conservative victories against common situs picketing and the labor law "reform" bill. Reed is an organizational genius who understands how to effectively use direct mail, newspaper ads, and other mass media techniques. Henry L. (Huck) Walther is vice president of membership services and largely responsible for the organization's meteoric growth from 25,000 to its present 1.5 million plus contributors and supporters. I predict Reed's efforts will persuade several new states to pass Right to Work laws in the next few years.

• Edwin Feulner is president of the Heritage Foundation, which has become the indispensable think tank for conservatives in Congress and opinion leaders across the nation. Heritage was started in 1973 by Paul Weyrich with major financial help from industrialist Joseph Coors, a courageous conservative. In the last four years under Feulner, Heritage has developed an amazing ability to get the right information to the right people at the right time.

It has gone from an annual budget in 1977 of less than $1 million to more than $4 million in 1980. Heritage now has 55 employees, including research experts on domestic and foreign affairs, and such resident scholars as Russell Kirk and Robert Conquest, the well-known British author.

Essential to Heritage's fast-reacting operation is its key location in three federal townhouses on Capitol Hill, only five blocks from the Capitol itself. Analyses and backgrounders on current bills are hand-delivered to members of Congress—sometimes within a day of their introduction. Its highly respected quarterly, *Policy*

Review, has been quoted by nearly every major columnist in the nation and used as the basis for thousands of newspaper editorials.

- Daniel J. Popeo is executive director of the Washington Legal Foundation. Sometimes described as the New Right's Ralph Nader, Dan won an epic battle in late 1979 on behalf of Sen. Barry Goldwater when a federal judge ruled that President Carter had illegally stopped the U.S.-Taiwan defense treaty. (Unfortunately, the case was lost on appeal.) Besides Jimmy Carter, Dan Popeo has also taken to court the Democratic National Committee, the General Services Administration, the Federal Mining Enforcement and Safety Administration, and the Federal Election Commission.

- Kathy Teague is executive director of the American Legislative Exchange Council, whose membership includes 600 conservative state legislators. A major ALEC publication is its biennial *Sourcebook of State Legislation*. Tennessee State Rep. Dave Copeland got the idea for a state constitutional tax limitation from ALEC's *Sourcebook* and went on to make Tennessee the first state in the nation to pass such a constitutional amendment in March 1978.

- Lee Edwards, called by the *New York Times* in 1969 the "Voice of the Silent Majority," organized many of the conservative movement's major events in the nation's capital in the 1960s and early 1970s. Many of the leaders of the New Right were first introduced to each other by Lee or met at events organized by Lee. He was a pioneer in setting the format for the informal style of ad hoc conservative meetings. His luncheons held monthly in downtown D.C. have helped knit together a healthy conservative community. He was an original director of the Committee for Responsible Youth Politics and the first editor of *Conservative Digest*. He wrote the first biography of Ronald Reagan in 1967.

- Gregg Hilton is executive director of the Conservative Victory Fund. Guided by Gregg's near encyclopedic knowledge of campaign facts, the Fund has steadily increased its financial support of conservative candidates, giving $500,000 in 1980.

- Paul Brown is head of the Life Amendment Political Action Committee (LAPAC). Propelled by the Supreme Court's pro-abortion decision in 1973, pro-life forces in America have mushroomed until in 1978, they played a decisive role in the defeats of liberal Senators Dick Clark of Iowa and Tom McIntyre of New Hampshire.

- Judie Brown is president of American Life Lobby, which works in Congress on pro-life issues. She was formerly executive secretary of the National Right to Life Committee, working closely with the brilliant Dr. Mildred Jefferson. Mrs. Brown entered the fight early against the one-sided White House Conference on Families. She has also helped lead the grassroots attack on the federal Model Adoption Act.

- Peter B. Gemma is national director of the National Pro-Life Political Action Committee. Gemma runs the Washington, D.C. office of NPLPAC, headed by Father Charles Fiore, O.P., and his broad campaign experience brings a high level of political sophistication to the pro-life movement.

- David Denholm is president of the Public Service Research Council (PSRC), with its 150,000 plus supporters, fights the growing power of public employee unions. Denholm's special goal is protecting citizens from police, firemen's, and teachers' strikes and the effects of forced collective bargaining between government and public employee unions. PSRC led the successful fight against liberalizing the Hatch Act, which restricts political activity by federal government workers.

- Rhonda Stahlman is chairman of Conservatives Against Liberal Legislation (CALL), a New Right, multi-issue lobbying group which is developing heavy weight ability to influence the legislative process. Rhonda was an officer of the Committee for Responsible Youth Politics and then of the National Conservative Political Action Committee. A dedicated Christian activist, she played a major role in bringing fundamentalist leaders like Dr. Bob Billings, with whom she worked in Indiana, into the New Right.

- Lew Uhler is chairman of the National Tax Limitation Committee, which now claims more than 100

Congressional co-sponsors of its constitutional amendment limiting federal spending to a declining share of the gross national product. The Committee has 500,000 financial supporters and an annual budget of more than $5 million.

• And last, but certainly not least, there is Phyllis Schlafly, founder and national chairman of Stop ERA. Phyllis is also president of the Eagle Forum, a national organization of conservative women, author of nine books, syndicated columnist, former CBS Radio commentator, wife and mother of six children, an attorney, a debater without equal—the heart and soul of a women's movement which believes in family, God and country.

She and her determined group of housewives and mothers have taken on and defeated the entire U.S. establishment, including three U.S. presidents, the Congress, the news media, organized labor, the foundations, and every liberal group you can name, from Common Cause to the National Organization for Women.

Phyllis is an excellent example of a true leader.

Phyllis did not stop ERA by simply making speeches, debating, writing books, articles and newsletters.

Of course, she did all of these things and did them well, but conservatives have been doing these things for years and losing almost every battle.

Phyllis set out to organize the anti-ERA movement.

She called meetings of her state officers, and they developed strategy as to how they would present their testimony before an upcoming legislative hearing. They would develop ideas on how to get media attention. They would determine which legislators needed to receive hundreds of letters and phone calls.

They would call for mass meetings of their supporters on the steps of each state capitol.

In other words, they developed a plan of action to win and implemented their plan with intelligent and hard work.

If Phyllis had only engaged in debates, speech making and writing, ERA would be the 27th Amendment to the U.S. Constitution.

Phyllis Schlafly would be the first to say that ERA has been stopped because of tens of thousands of hard working women and men volunteers.

But without this brilliant leader calling meetings and organizing the opposition, a million volunteers could not have stopped the liberal juggernaut from passing ERA.

• I have already mentioned Dr. Jerry Falwell, who no longer needs any introduction to the American public. Later I will devote a special chapter to the born-again Christian movement.

• Closely related to the born-again movement (and sharing some leadership with it) is the pro-family movement. A later chapter will cover it too, but here I will mention a few of its more prominent leaders:

Senators Jake Garn and Orrin Hatch of Utah, Jesse Helms of North Carolina, Paul Laxalt of Nevada and Gordon Humphrey of New Hampshire, Congressmen John Ashbrook of Ohio, Philip Crane of Illinois, Robert Dornan of California, Henry Hyde of Illinois, Larry McDonald of Georgia, and Bob Walker of Pennsylvania.

Bill Billings, National Christian Action Coalition; Dr. Bob Billings, The Moral Majority; JoAnn Gasper, Right Woman; attorney William Ball; Fr. Virgil C. Blum, S.J., Catholic League for Religious and Civil Rights; Harry Covert, editor, *Moral Majority Report*; and Lottie Beth Hobbs, Pro-Family Forum.

Margaret Hotze, Life Advocates; June Larson, Citizens for Constructive Education; Ron Marr, *Christian Inquirer*; Rosemary Thomson, Family America; Martha Rountree, Leadership Foundation; Wayne Allen, Briarcrest Baptist School System (Memphis); and John Beckett, Intercessors for America.

Tim and Beverly LaHaye; Paige Patterson, Criswell Institute of Biblical Studies (Dallas); Ross Rhoads, Calvary Presbyterian Church (Charlotte); LaNeil Wright, Esther Action Council; Fr. Morton Hill, S.J., Morality in Media, and Fletcher Brothers, Gates Community Chapel (Rochester, N.Y.).

Randy Engel, U.S. Coalition for Life; Nellie Gray, March for Life; Patrick A. Trueman, Americans United for Life; and Ohio State Sen. Donald E. (Buz) Lukens, Americans for Life.

There are dozens of conservative movement activists in public office—in the U.S. Senate, in the U.S. House of

Representatives and in state legislatures across the nation. I cannot list them all, but here are a few who are always seeking to build the conservative movement—who have taken a leadership role in crucial New Right battles—who are determined not just to put up a good fight but to win:

• Senator Orrin G. Hatch of Utah. A former tax lawyer and union member, Orrin led the successful battles against labor law "reform," IRS harassment of Christian schools and federal funding of abortions.

• Senator Jesse A. Helms of North Carolina. I feel that just as Robert Taft was known as Mr. Republican, we will soon see Jesse Helms become known as Mr. Conservative. Jesse *is* the conscience of the conservative movement. He has introduced an amendment permitting prayer in public schools which may soon become law. He led the battle against Senate rules changes that would have strengthened the majority leader's power. He has commanded countless foreign policy battles, including Rhodesia, Nicaragua and Taiwan. He initiated the campaign to grant honorary U.S. citizenship to Alexander Solzhenitsyn. He has a number of important movement conservatives on his staff, such as Dr. James Lucier and John Carbaugh, who have gained national reputations.

• Sen. Paul Laxalt of Nevada. He was the very effective leader in our battle against Senate ratification of the Panama Canal treaties, winning praise for his grace and good humor from friend and foe alike. He was national chairman for Ronald Reagan's presidential campaign in 1976 and again in 1980. He also led the fight against instant voter registration and taxpayer financing of Congressional elections.

• Sen. James McClure of Idaho. As chairman of the influential Senate Steering Committee, McClure speaks softly but carries a big stick. He has made a specialty of energy, exposing the elitism of the environmental movement and the fanaticism of the anti-nuclear forces.

• Congressman Philip Crane of Illinois. Phil waged a tireless campaign for the Republican nomination for President from 1978-80, carrying the conservative message to millions of Americans. He chaired the American

Conservative Union from 1977-1979, during the period of its greatest growth. As ACU chairman, he organized and hosted monthly ecumenical luncheons which greatly helped old and new conservatives to work out their personal tactics and strategy differences. A major factor in Phil's effectiveness was Rich Williamson, who was Phil's principal political adviser for many years and who continues to contribute significantly to the conservative movement.

• Congressman Robert Dornan of California, an electrifying public speaker who originated the idea for the POW-MIA bracelet in 1970 when he was a Los Angeles broadcaster. Over 5 million bracelets were distributed. Congressman Dornan was active in stopping the transfer of Cyber 76 advanced computers to Soviet Russia and has fought hard for the B-1 bomber.

• Congressman Mickey Edwards of Oklahoma, who followed Winston Churchill's advice to never, never give up. Mickey ran and narrowly lost in 1974, receiving 48.3% of the vote. He ran and won narrowly in 1976, receiving almost exactly half the vote. But he put it all together in 1978, winning reelection with 80% of the vote, including over 75% of the black and labor vote. And in 1981, Congressman Edwards became chairman of the American Conservative Union.

• Congressman Newt Gingrich of Georgia, who has emerged as a principal spokesman for the conservative coalition in Congress. Gingrich showed his leadership ability in November 1979 when he organized bi-partisan support for an alternative to the White House-Speaker Tip O'Neill budget. He narrowly lost by a vote of 205-190, an impressive showing for a freshman Republican against the combined power of the White House, Speaker O'Neill and the rest of the Democratic leadership.

• Senator Steve Symms of Idaho. Steve is a libertarian conservative who defeated Sen. Frank Church in 1980. A farmer who practices free enterprise, Steve is an American who understands the importance of maintaining peace and security through strength.

• Democratic Congressman Larry McDonald is from Jimmy Carter's Georgia, but he voted against Carter more than any other Member in the 95th Congress. Larry is always out in front on domestic and national security issues and is pressing to restore the House Internal Security Committee. He is dedicated to building the conservative movement nationally and is generous in the giving of his time and talent.

• California State Sen. H. L. (Bill) Richardson founded both Gun Owners of America and Gun Owners of California in 1975 and has built them into highly effective political operations. Together the organizations have over a hundred thousand supporters and annual budgets of more than a million dollars.

You may notice a missing element here: big business. I'd like to say something here about the so-called support of conservative causes by big business. As far as the New Right is concerned, it never existed.

It is not true that what is good for General Motors is good for the country — or that what is good for big business is automatically good for conservatives.

The New Right rejects both propositions. This is one of the things that distinguishes us from the Republican establishment. It may also help explain why that establishment even more than the liberal Democrats sold this country a bill of goods labelled détente.

The truth is that big business has become far too cozy with big government. In fact, big government protects big business. It's a sweetheart arrangement. Big business is comfortable with red tape, regulations, bureaucracy— these things freeze the status quo, impede newcomers, and hold down competition.

We've seen so-called believers in free enterprise like Lockheed and Chrysler run crying to Congress for bailouts to save them from their own bad business decisions.

We've seen business and association PACs make big contributions to incumbent liberal congressmen while ignoring promising conservative challengers.

We've seen big business spend millions on advertising in pornographic publications like *Playboy*, *Hustler* and *Penthouse* without any regard for the impact on our greatest national resource—our young people.

We've seen big business eager to trade with the Communist enemies not only of capitalism but of religious liberty, family life, and of all forms of privacy and personal freedom. Not only is big business often heedless of moral principles, it is often willing to contribute to the Soviet war machine's threat to America and the free world, selling the Soviets the means to destroy us.

No, big business can't take our support for granted. They'll have to earn it. Despite its enormous material productiveness, the business community as a whole has proved itself lacking in the moral fiber America so desperately needs in order to survive and prosper.

So there you have a profile of the New Right's leadership. As you can see, it is tremendously diverse—like America herself.

Our cooperation is completely voluntary. We have no bosses or "Godfathers." Our unity lies in harmony of purpose. This, and not centralized control, is our way— as we believe it's the American way.

At the same time, we can't afford to forget our common goals in the pursuit of our independent aims. George Bush is a fine American, but he would not have been the Vice-Presidential preference of the New Right. He holds that office today—and may be President tomorrow—in part because the New Right could not agree on an alternative candidate.

We should live by the words of Williams James: "A small force, if it never lets up, will accumulate effects more considerable than those of much greater forces if these work inconsistently."

X

Our Primary Goal: Military Superiority

At one time, there was no "conservative" position on defense. Everyone agreed that America should be strong, certainly strong enough to contain the Soviet Union. The only debate was between those who wanted to "roll back" Communism and those who would settle for "containing" it.

Things have come to such a pass that either of these positions now places you at the conservative end of the political spectrum. The Left has tried to corner and isolate anyone who spoke out for a powerful America.

It has backfired. Today it is the Left that is isolated. If there is one thing the vast majority of Americans agree on, it's that we can't afford to be weak in today's world. By branding this a rightist position, the Left handed the Right one of the most potent issues around—an issue that unites and energizes millions of Americans, social conservatives, fiscal conservatives, moderates, and those moderate liberals who have refused to go leftward with their peers.

All these people realize that it's idle to talk about their goals and ideals unless America's survival is assured.

And they agree that our survival has become a real question.

How bad off are we?

By all standards—overall spending, strategic air weapons, naval forces, ground forces—we have fallen far behind the Soviets.

• In military manpower, Soviet Russia has armed forces of 4 million. We have about 2 million men and women, all volunteer.

• They have close to 50,000 tanks, we have 10,500. They have about 20,000 field artillery, we have some 6,000.

• The Soviets have an estimated 3,736 strategic offensive weapons, including ICBMs, SLBMs, cruise missiles and manned bombers. We have 2,124 such offensive weapons.

• They have 14,664 strategic defensive weapons, including SAMs and fighter planes. We have 309, repeat, 309 such defensive weapons.

• The Soviets have 594 major ships and submarines. We have 296 such vessels.

• Since the early 1970's, Soviet Russia has been spending three times as much as the U.S. on strategic weapons alone.

• In 1978, the Defense Nuclear Agency estimated that Soviet Russia was ahead of the United States in 33 of 41 categories of strategic power.

Clearly, we have fallen from being the Number One military power in the world to the Number Two power— behind a country whose leaders are totally committed to defeating America and conquering the world.

Liberal presidents and liberal Congresses have deliberately put us in second place, believing that America's overwhelming strength was a threat to the Soviets and world peace.

In *The Eleventh Hour*, General Lewis W. Walt former commandant of the U.S. Marine Corps, explains how it happened:

"The triad of weapons which provided us with a shield against both nuclear war and nuclear blackmail was based on land-based missiles, submarine-launched missiles and strategic bombers. . .

110

"(But) our strategic triad has aged and lost its ability to deter war.

"The president and a majority in congress have refused to replace the B-52 (bomber), designed in 1948; they have delayed building a mobile missile system; they have scrapped our air defense and civil defense; they have delayed the neutron warhead; and they have frozen the third leg of the triad, the nuclear subs, by diplomatic agreement."

In 1965, Defense Secretary Robert McNamara established this disarmament policy when he declared: "The Soviets have decided that they have lost the quantitative race . . . there is no indication the Soviets are seeking to develop a strategic nuclear force as large as ours."

Such dangerous misjudgments by the liberals have resulted in unilateral disarmament by America while the Soviets have forged ahead of us in every military category. Liberals, in effect, have issued an open invitation to increased Soviet aggression around the world.

The basic problem is that most liberals refuse to believe that the Communists are really working to conquer the world. In the 1930's most leaders in democratic countries (with a few exceptions like Winston Churchill and Douglas MacArthur) refused to believe that the Germans and the Japanese had any intention of conquering the world. Yet Hitler explained his plans in detail in his book, *Mein Kampf*, published in 1925.

European leaders ignored Hitler until too late. As a result, more than 25 million babies, children, women and men paid with their lives and hundreds of millions more suffered through the death and serious injury of their loved ones or the destruction of their homes and property during Hitler's war in Europe.

The major Communist leaders have written hundreds of books, and made millions of speeches declaring their ultimate goal of completely destroying capitalism and freedom. Yet, the vast majority of the leaders of the free world (most of them liberals) still refuse to believe the Communists.

Maybe I could understand why the liberals refuse to believe conservatives, but this question demands an answer:

Given the 64-year record of the Communists, why do so many liberals still refuse to believe those farther left

on the political spectrum—the Communists?
Consider the Communists' own words.

- Lenin: "We stand for permanent revolution."

- Lenin: "As long as capitalism and socialism exist, we cannot live in peace: in the end, one or the other will triumph—a funeral dirge will be sung either over the Soviet Republic or over world capitalism."

- Stalin: "Can the capitalists be forced out and the roots of capitalism be annihilated without a bitter class struggle? No, it is impossible."

- Mao Tse-tung: "Every Communist must grasp that political power grows out of the barrel of a gun . . . . In fact, we can say that the whole world can be remolded only with a gun."

- Khrushchev: "I can prophesy that your grand-children in America will live under socialism"

- Khrushchev: "We will bury you."

- Brezhnev: "We are achieving with detente what our predecessors have been unable to achieve using the mailed fist . . . . (By 1985) we will have consolidated our position. We will have improved our economy. And a decisive shift in the correlation of forces will be such that, come 1985, we will be able to exert our will whenever we need to."

- Brezhnev: "Our aim is to gain control of the two great houses on which the West depends—the energy treasure of the Persian Gulf and the mineral treasure house of central and southern Africa."
Consider the Communists' 63-year record of conquest.

- 1917: Russia

- 1920: Armenia, Azerbaijan, Byelorussia, Coassackia, Udel-Ural, North Caucasia, Georgia, the Ukraine.

- 1922: the Far Eastern Republic, Turkestan.

- 1924: the Mongolian People's Republic.

- 1940: Estonia, Latvia, Lithuania.

- 1945: Yugoslavia.

- 1946: Albania, Bulgaria.

112

- 1947: Poland, Rumania.
- 1948: Czechoslovakia, North Korea.
- 1949: Hungary, East Germany, Mainland China.
- 1951: Tibet.
- 1954: North Vietnam
- Cuba

Consider also their record of conquest over the last six years—the era of "detente."

- 1974-5: Ethiopia.
- 1975: South Vietnam, Cambodia.
- 1976: Angola, Mozambique.
- 1977: Laos.
- 1978: South Yemen.
- 1979: Afghanistan.

Consider the human cost of Communism.

British journalist D.G. Stewart-Smith, in his book *Defeat of Communism*, estimated that from 1917 to 1964, international Communism was directly responsible for the death of 83 million people—excluding World War II. More than 45 million deaths were in Soviet Russia through civil war, famines, purges, slave labor camps and the "liquidation" of the peasant farmers.

American expert Richard Walker has estimated in an official document for the U.S. Senate that at least 32 million and possibly as many as 62 million Chinese died as a result of Communism in China.

Alexander Solzhenitsyn has eloquently described the human cost of Communism in the Soviet slave camps in his epic, *The Gulag Archipelago*.

In his definitive work, *Workers Paradise Lost*, Eugene Lyons wrote that "no fewer than 50 million Soviet citizens" lived and usually died in Soviet labor camps.

In view of the Communists' bloody record and in view of the liberals' apparent inability to acknowledge it, I can't help but wonder:

Do the liberals really deserve their reputation of having great compassion and concern for their fellow men?

To put it bluntly, we are locked in world-wide combat with Communism. In fact, as British strategic expert Brian Crozier has written, we have been fighting the Third World War since before the Second World War ended.

Yes, even before the end of the fighting in Europe and the Pacific, Joseph Stalin was laying plans for Communist domination of his neighbors. The Soviet armies that pursued the retreating Nazis into Eastern Europe stayed and imposed Communism on the peoples of Poland, Hungary, Czechoslovakia, Yugoslavia, Rumania, Bulgaria, Albania and East Germany.

Stalin later commented: "The reason why there is now no Communist government in Paris is because in the circumstance of 1945 the Soviet Army was not able to reach French soil."

For the last third of a century, the Communists have continued to wage war while the Free World has followed a policy of so-called "containment" which has failed.

In the last 63 years more than 1.8 billion men, women and children have been taken, not by their choice, behind the ever-expanding Iron, Bamboo and Sugar Cane Curtains.

Meanwhile, America has indeed become, in the words of former President Richard Nixon, "a pitiful helpless giant."

But it was Nixon and former Secretary of State Henry Kissinger who were responsible for the policy of detente which helped make us pitiful and helpless.

And detente prepared the way for Jimmy Carter's incredible 1977 speech at Notre Dame when he declared that America had entered "a new world" freed from "that inordinate fear of Communism" which led three U.S. Presidents into the "moral poverty" of Vietnam.

Carter revealed his true bent by stopping the B-1 bomber . . . sending a U.S. diplomatic mission to Cuba . . . promising to abide by SALT II, even if the Senate refused to ratify it . . . trying to remove U.S. ground troops from South Korea . . . supporting the Soviet-backed Patriotic Front in Rhodesia . . . denouncing small right-wing countries such as South Africa and Chile for alleged violations of human rights but ignoring massive murder and oppression of human beings in left-wing countries such as Cuba, Vietnam, Communist China and Soviet Russia.

The Soviet invasion of Afghanistan did shake up Jimmy Carter, causing him to say on December 31, 1979: "My opinion of the Russians has changed more drastically in the last week than even the previous 2½ years before that."

You can't help but wonder as columnist George Will wrote a week later: "How serious is change brought on by a 55-year-old man suddenly noticing a 62-year-old reality, the nature of Soviet statecraft?"

But within a few weeks, Carter showed his old spots by insisting that SALT II was still needed. And he has been far less than candid about the so-called halting of U.S. exports to Russia because of Afghanistan.

According to Lawrence Brady, formerly of the Department of Commerce, the Carter embargo affected only 7% of our exports to the Soviet Union.

Brady actually lost his job in the Commerce Department (over the protests of the Merit Systems Protection Board, a federal commission set up to protect whistleblowers) because he exposed the fraudulence of that embargo.

Untouched, for example, was a Diesel engine assembly line made by Ingersoll-Rand for the Soviet Kama River plant, the largest truck plant in the world. Many of its trucks are outfitted for use as missile carriers, armed personnel carriers, and command vehicles. Some of these have been reliably reported as in use now—in Afghanistan.

I can remember back in the 1960s that conservative groups like Young Americans for Freedom were able to get Firestone not to trade with the Communists through picket lines and other action projects. I thought that after Russia invaded Afghanistan that it was time once again to use a boycott and similar tactics against any nation which is not on our side in the continuing struggle against Communism.

Jimmy Carter did call for a boycott of the Moscow Olympics. But he failed, as usual, to put enough pressure on our major allies to follow our example. He was unable to lead, once again.

That's why I called for a boycott of products made in France, Italy, and Eastern European countries such as

East Germany, Poland and Czechoslovakia not supporting our boycott of the Olympics.

Now that we have a new President and Secretary of State, who have promised bolder action and stronger leadership in our relations with Russia, I feel we should give the nations who went to the Moscow Olympics a chance for a fresh start and end the boycott.

American businessmen have long helped supply strategic equipment for the Soviet war machine. Consider a few examples:

• *Precision grinders.* In 1972, the Soviets obtained 164 Centalign-B ball-bearing grinder machines, manufactured by the Bryant Chucking Grinder Company. Four years later, Defense Intelligence Agency officials told Congress that the grinders "may now be used in the guidance equipment of Soviet missiles."

• *Oil drilling technology.* In the fall of 1978, the Carter administration approved 74 export licenses, including a $144 million oil drill bit factory by Dresser Industries. The sale involved the transfer of an electronic beam welding machine that can be used to make jet aircraft and might also have nuclear and laser applications.

• *Computers.* U.S. computer sales to the Soviet Union have run into hundreds of millions of dollars. Dr. Miles Costick, a leading defense analyst and author, has noted that the export of American computers, including the Control Data Cyber 73 and the IBM 370/145, 370/155 and 370/158 to Moscow "will enhance Soviet strategic capabilities across the board."

In 1977, then FBI Director Clarence Kelley told an industrial association that "businessmen who sell technology to the Soviet bloc are making a tragic mistake." He pleaded with U.S. businessmen to put "patriotism over profit, knowledge over naiveté."

But it appears that many big businessmen don't care what happens tomorrow as long as they make a sale today.

Lenin was correct when he reportedly said that capitalists would sell the Communists the rope to hang themselves.

In fact, most of the Communist countries pay for products bought from American corporations by credit. But the American big businessman takes almost no risk because the Communist credit is guaranteed by the American government.

That means that you the taxpayer are making it possible for big American corporations to make a profit selling truck factories, computers and oil drilling equipment to the Communists—just as they did in the 1930's when American corporations sold scrap iron to Japan that was later used to kill Americans in World War II.

The alarming surge in Communist debt to Western countries and banks since the start of detente is a serious problem for the Free World.

By the end of 1979, the Soviet bloc owed an estimated $75 billion to Western governments and banks— up from $17.6 billion in 1973.

There is real doubt about the Communists' ability or intention to repay their debts. And the size of their debt gives the Communists enormous power. There's an old saying: "Make a small loan and you have a debtor; make a large loan and you have created a partner."

For an example of the danger of large loans, look at how U.S. bankers lobbied strongly for the Panama Canal treaties. Could it have been because of Panama's $2.4 billion dollar debt to the bankers?

And Moscow's black record of consistently breaking treaties make the chances of its repaying its financial debts very questionable.

V.I. Lenin is the final authority for all good Communists on how to conduct themselves. Here is what Lenin said in 1918 about agreements: "It is ridiculous not to know that a treaty is a means of gaining strength."

While Stalin, his successor for 29 years, said about diplomatic lying: "A diplomat's words must have no relation to action—otherwise, what kind of diplomacy is it?

"Words are one thing, actions another. Good words are a mask for the concealment of bad deeds. Sincere diplomacy is no more possible than dry water or iron wood."

Dr. Igor Glagolev, a member of the Soviet negotiating team for SALT who defected to the United States, has described the Russians' real intentions this way:

"In the period of the talks on SALT I (signed in 1972), the Brezhnev-Andropov leadership of the USSR took the following decisions:

"—to achieve an overwhelming military superiority over the United States, a superiority sufficient to win not only conventional wars in different parts of the world but also an all-out nuclear war;

"—to conceal this superiority from the public with the help of the censorship in the USSR and the pro-Soviet media in the West;

"—to establish Soviet influence in Indochina and Africa with the help of local Communist or pro-Communist forces organized and armed by the Soviet Union;

"—to break the agreement on peace in Vietnam and the Helsinki agreements."

Can anyone deny that this is precisely and exactly what the Soviets have done in the last eight years?

Yet the Third World War is not over. It can still be won by the Free World if we take certain critical steps without delay.

The first and most important is to abandon detente which has been a disaster for the West. Dr. Paul Eidelberg, an American foreign policy analyst, has outlined just how disastrous in his remarkable book, *Beyond Detente: Toward An American Foreign Policy*. According to Dr. Eidelberg, detente has only negative consequences for the West. It dignifies Soviet rulers. It discourages internal resistance within the Soviet Union and freedom movements in the satellites. It enables Moscow to divide and undermine NATO by means of bilateral agreements with individual members of the alliance. It weakens the will to resist Communism and lulls the Free World into complacency.

Detente, Dr. Eidelberg argues and I agree, is not a policy of peace but one of appeasement which increases the likelihood of nuclear war.

In place of detente we need a policy of military superiority over the Communists (history shows that superior military strength is the best way to prevent war with an aggressor country) combined with a multi-billion dollar effort to fight the Communists with propaganda in every country of the world.

As George Washington said, "The best way to insure peace is to be prepared for war."

A number of leading conservative experts, including Dr. Eidelberg, General Daniel Graham, Brian Crozier of London, Congressman Jack Kemp and General Lewis A.

Walt, have proposed in their books and articles what might be called a victory policy. No, these distinguished authorities do not recommend a nuclear attack on the Soviet Union. But they do urge that the United States and the Free World adopt a political, economic, diplomatic *offensive* against Communism.

Here is a summary of major conservative proposals on foreign policy and national defense:

• Regain strategic military superiority without delay.

• Stop any technology, capital investments or loans which could advance, directly or indirectly, the war-making power of the Soviet Union.

• Expose and condemn Soviet violations of international agreements and laws.

• Develop the conventional military power necessary to respond to the various kinds of Soviet-supported aggression.

• Use diplomatic devices like recalling our ambassador and severing diplomatic relations when the Soviets use force against their satellites or other nations as they did to Czechoslovakia in 1968 and Afghanistan in 1979.

• Free America from arms control restraints which perpetuate U.S. military inferiority and force us to fight the Third World War by Soviet rules.

Anthony Dolan, winner of a Pulitzer Prize for journalism in 1978, a special assistant to campaign director William Casey in the Reagan presidential effort, and now a speech writer for President Reagan, suggested some foreign policy initiatives in *National Review* in May 1980. They dealt with Soviet weakness in an important but frequently neglected area—captive nations. Dolan proposed:

• The U.S. ambassador to the United Nations bring before the General Assembly a demand for the removal of the Soviet occupation forces in Eastern Europe as well as Afghanistan. The ambassador would back up his demand with the facts about Soviet invasion and suppression for over 30 years of the peoples of Hungary, Czechoslovakia, Poland, etc.

• The White House would announce a new form of "linkage"—including in any future diplomatic negotiations with Moscow the demand for Soviet withdrawal from Eastern Europe.

• A call for troop removal and free elections not only in Eastern Europe but the Baltic nations of Latvia, Estonia and Lithuania and the non-Russian republics of Ukraine, Georgia, Turkistan and so forth. Such demands, as Dolan pointed out, would focus UN debates not on "absurd discussions of colonialism in the Virgin Islands and Puerto Rico" but on the critical issue of this century—Soviet Russian imperialism.

We should also:

• Increase and expand anti-Communist propaganda and information, with special attention focused on Radio Free Europe and Radio Liberty. There is no good reason why we should not spend as much time and effort stirring up trouble behind the Iron Curtain as the Soviets spend trying to undermine our domestic system.

Dr. Fred Schawrz argues that with 1% of the U.S. military budget, about $1.8 billion, propaganda "miracles could be wrought." An "army of authors and translators," in Dr. Schawrz' words, could be recruited and set to work producing material about the doctrines, history and objectives of Communism.

Printing companies could produce literature in every language designed for every segment of the world's population. Messages could be produced for radio broadcast. Films could be made and distributed to every corner of the world.

Says Dr. Schwarz: "The change in the world scene would be dramatic. The advance of communism would stop."

We should also:

• Rebuild our security and intelligence-gathering capability. We need the Defense Intelligence Agency, the CIA and the National Security Agency abroad and the

FBI at home to let us know what our enemies are doing.

For example, there was a 99% drop in domestic security cases in the mid-70's, from 21,414 to just 214 in 1977. Meanwhile, 1,900 registered Soviet bloc officials went about their spy business and thousands of potential terrorists (as reported in *Conservative Digest* in October 1977) prepared for their next bombing or kidnapping.

We should also:

• Strengthen U.S. alliances, particularly friends and allies not only in Western Europe but in Latin America, southern Africa and Asia.

• Support pro-Western forces under Soviet-sponsored attack. We helped preserve the peace in Europe, the Middle East and Northeastern Africa in the 1940s and 1950s. Our recent record has been far less impressive in Angola, Mozambique, Ethiopia and Southeast Asia.

• Accept the heavy burden of international leadership. As Brian Crozier has warned, "Unless a new awareness and alertness are fostered, and unless the right action is taken in time, then the way of life that is under threat is indeed doomed—not by any law of 'historical inevitability' as the Marxist might suppose, but by internal demoralization and a loss of will to face the threats from without and within."

"A loss of will." How often that phrase is used by conservative experts as they analyze why the Free World has failed to meet the challenge of Communism. The ability to act counts for little unless it is accompanied by the willingness to act.

And always there is the element of time. Before 1963, it took about six years to translate an idea into a weapons system. Now it takes an estimated 15 years. In other words, the MX missile, a needed counterforce weapon, will not be ready for another 10 years if we proceed at our present pace.

I believe we must return to a World War II emergency method of rebuilding our military position. That would mean doing away with time-consuming purchasing requirements, arms control impact statements, low bids, and any EPA or OSHA rules that hampered production.

It would mean keeping some plants open 24 hours a day. It would mean a total commitment by everyone from the President to the worker on the job and a realization that we are at war with a dangerous enemy.

In the early 1940s when we had to build an arsenal or watch Germany and Japan conquer the world, the United States amazed friend and foe alike by setting production records never seen before or since.

As the old song goes, "We did it before and we can do it again." But today, we have much less time.

The alternative to such an all-out American effort is simple. The Soviets will either force us into a war we will lose or we will be forced to surrender.

RAV and evangelist Jerry Falwell.

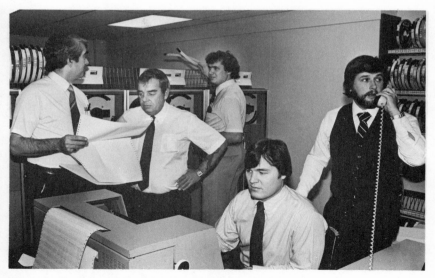

Viguerie Co. computer executives working on a mailing.
l to r: Chuck Gardner, Bill Smith, Mark O'Connor, Andy Kuhrtz, Ron Brooks

Ronald Reagan and RAV look over an issue of *Conservative Digest.*

Paul Brown, director of LAPAC, Mrs. Fob James (the wife of Alabama's governor) and Ed McAteer, chairman of The Religious Roundtable.

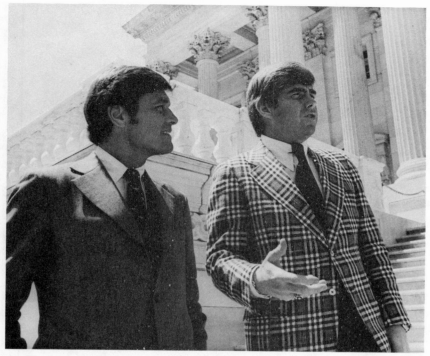

Congressman Philip Crane and Jack Kemp on the U.S. Capitol steps.

Terry Dolan, Sen. Gordon Humphery and Congressman Jerry Solomon on the trip to Taiwan.

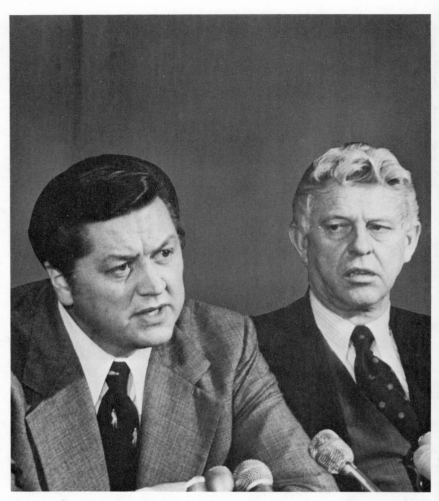

Congressman George Hansen and Lt. Gen. Daniel Graham (USA) Ret. brief
news media on Panama Canal Truth Squad objectives, February, 1978.

The Vigueries host a party at their home honoring Senator Hatch.
r to l: Elaine Viguerie, Senator Hatch, RAV, Sue Edwards, Congressman
Mickey Edwards.

Congressmen Norm Shumway, William Dannemeyer and Mickey Edwards and
Warren Richardson being briefed by Bill Rhatican on the way to Taiwan.

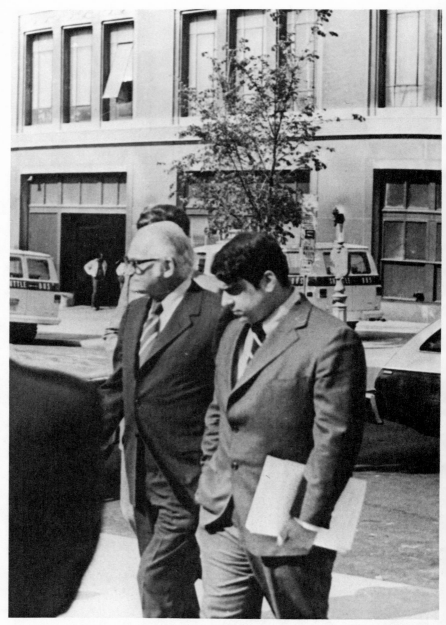

Sen. Barry Goldwater and Dan Popeo of the Washington Legal Foundation on their way to court to challenge President Carter's cancelling of the U.S.-Republic of China mutual defense treaty.

Holly Coors, Joseph Coors, Ed Feulner and Glenn Campbell, director of the Hoover Institution, at the dedication of the Holly and Joseph Coors Building of the Heritage Foundation.

Sen. James McClure, Howard Phillips and Sen. Jesse Helms at the Conservative Caucus 5th anniversary celebration.

Congressman Larry McDonald and Paul Weyrich on the Panama Canal Truth Squad Plane.

l to r: Richard Viguerie's mother, Elizabeth, and father, Arthur; Elaine Viguerie's father, Joseph O'Leary and mother, Adela.

Milton Friedman, Ed Feulner and Rose Friedman at Heritage headquarters in Washington.

British Prime Minister Margaret Thatcher and Right to Work Committee President Reed Larson.

RAV, son Ryan, and daughters Renée and Michelle on a family outing, Septamber, 1978.

RAV, actor Pat Boone and Congressman Robert Dornan at a Dornan for Congress fundraising dinner held at the Viguerie's home.

RAV, Howard Phillips, William Rhatican and Congressman Mickey Edwards
aboard the Panama Canal Truth Squad Plane.

Connaught Marshner, chairman, Library Court.

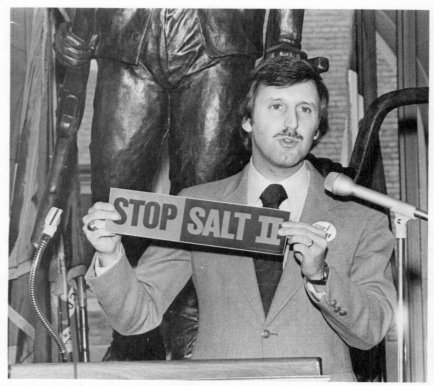

Bob Heckman, executive director of YAF, displays bumper sticker from their "Stop SALT II" campaign.

Gregg Hilton, executive director, Conservative Victory Fund.

David Denholm, Public Service Research Council, John Laxalt, Citizens for the Republic, and Charlie Black, New Right leader.

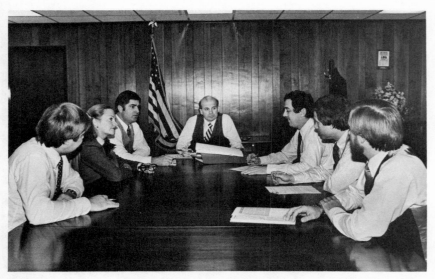

RAV reviews advertising campaign with Viguerie Co. vice presidents, Ann Stone, Jim Aldigé, Tom Kilpatrick, Steve Peck and Hugh Chewning and at the far left Earl Chester, president of American Mailing List Co.

Iowa Lt. Gov. Terry Branstad and Kathy Teague, ALEC executive director, at an ALEC meeting.

Bill Faulkner, Jerry Falwell and Dr. Bob Billings of the Moral Majority.

Margo Carlisle, Senate Steering Committee executive director, with Senators James McClure and Gordon Humphrey.

Paul Weyrich, CSFC director, and wife Joyce; RAV and Elaine; Sen. Paul Laxalt and wife Carol at a dinner when plaques were given to Senator Laxalt and RAV for their successful efforts to stop taxpayer financing of Congressional elections.

Lee Edwards and William F. Buckley, Jr. backstage at a Washington conservative conference.

Conservatives throw a surprise 40th birthday party for Morton Blackwell. r to l: Mrs. Wm. G. Blackwell, Wm. G. Blackwell, Mrs. Charles Reddy, Morton Blackwell, Helen Blackwell, Richard Dingman, M. Stanton Evans.

XI

The Born-Again Christian
Discovers Politics

In 1976 Jimmy Carter helped make born-again Christians a national political force, and they helped elect him. But by 1980 he had lost their support—and they helped replace him with Ronald Reagan.

When Jimmy Carter campaigned for President in 1976, he put together a coalition (much as Franklin D. Roosevelt did 44 years earlier) of widely different groups: union officials, blacks, McGovern activists, environmentalists, Naderites and fundamentalist Christians.

Carter had been elected only a few hours when most of these groups were bragging loudly how their support had made the difference between winning and losing.

But one group made very little noise about their support of Jimmy Carter—the born-again Christians. They remained quiet despite the fact that they probably gave Carter more votes than any other single category of people.

Jimmy Carter received almost the same percentage of the black vote in 1976 (93%) as George McGovern did in 1972 (92%).

And while I was not able to find any reliable figures as to how many millions of born-again Christians voted for Nixon or Wallace in 1968 and for Nixon in 1972, but switched to Carter in 1976, I think it's fair to say that between 5 million and 7.5 million switched.

So it's clear that the born-again Christians were much more important to Jimmy Carter than the blacks. And it's also clear that the blacks can be assumed to always vote for the Democratic candidate regardless of who the nominee is. Even George Wallace running against a racially moderate Republican for Governor of Alabama in 1974 received a majority of the black vote.

So the blacks have sent a message loud and clear to the politicians—they are Democrats and, regardless of the candidate, they will vote Democrat.

But the born-again Christians clearly are not married to any political party as are the blacks, union officials, environmentalists and Naderites.

In light of these facts, it's difficult to understand why for four years, Carter gave the born-again Christians the back of his hand.

The blacks, the McGovern supporters, Ralph Nader and his follower, the environmentalists, all let President Carter know almost daily that they supported him in 1976 and that they wanted their just rewards.

But the born-again Christians asked for nothing but to be left alone.

And what was Jimmy Carter's response to his biggest and most important single issue group of supporters?

Not only did the Carter administration ignore the born-again Christians, it actively and aggressively sought to hurt the Christian movement in America.

For example, the IRS, whose head was appointed by Carter and can be removed by Carter, made a major effort to put the Christian school movement out of business by saying that most private schools started after 1953 are presumed to be "racist" until they meet quotas proposed by IRS. A "racist" school would lose its tax-deductible status, which means it would most likely have to shut its doors. Pressure put on Congress in 1980 by New Right groups caused it to pass legislation, effectively preventing the IRS from implementing this policy.

For example, Carter and his aides have indicated that if Congress passed a law that would allow voluntary prayer in public schools he would veto it.

For another example, Carter appointed to high government office only a few clearly identified fundamantalist Christians. Instead, he surrounded himself with many people who routinely rejected Biblical principles regarding sexual behavior, family responsibility, abortion and other key moral issues.

It is hard to believe that Carter was so callous to his most important and biggest supporters of 1976. But it's true. No wonder they voted for Ronald Reagan in 1980.

He had a golden opportunity in July and August 1979 when he made wholesale changes in his cabinet to try and get back in the good graces of born-again Christians, moral majority Americans, and fed-up taxpayers.

But Carter ignored these groups. Instead, he drew his appointments from the same old crowd of liberals and big businessmen—picking people like Patricia Harris, G. William Miller, Moon Landrieu and Neil Goldschmidt.

Two of the most basic rules of politics are that you must have a base of support and you must protect that base of support.

But Carter did not even know what his real base of support was. He obviously thought it was the union officials, the environmentalists, the McGovern liberals in the Democratic Party.

But as he learned in the primaries during the first half of 1980, a large chunk of that liberal-labor coalition backed Teddy Kennedy.

Carter also wrapped the American flag around him with his failed attempt to rescue the American hostages in Iran, his tough talk regarding the Soviets and his call for more defense spending. It's probable that Carter survived Kennedy and even kept a neo-conservative out of the Democratic race with his "tough" patriotic talk in the last part of 1979 and first half of 1980.

But all these unhappy groups in America—the taxpayer, the born-again Christian, the pro-defense citizen, the moral majority American—actively looked for an alternative to Jimmy Carter.

Government assaults on church rights weren't all that bothered conservative Christians.

Government attacks on the family, like the Supreme Court's original 1973 pro-abortion decision, the Equal Rights Amendment, plans to draft women, and various homosexual rights ordinances also concerned them.

As a result, conservative Christians—particularly fundamentalist Protestants—got politically involved.

Evangelists like Jerry Falwell, James Robison, and Pat Robertson, who reach over 20 million people by television every week, talked about political issues and urged their listeners to register to vote and get involved in politics.

Separation of church and state, they reminded their audiences, does not mean separation of God and government.

"The only hope for America," says Rev. Falwell, "is to awaken the religious people of America." He adds that preachers must get involved in politics since the "leadership of godly men is the best available."

Rev. Falwell practices what he preaches. He has probably done more than any other person to block passage of ERA in Virginia.

Reflecting the deep patriotism of most evangelists, Rev. Falwell organized in July 1979 a 12,000-person pro-American rally on the steps of the U.S. Capitol. Among the New Right leaders who addressed the rally were Sen. Jesse Helms, Sen. Gordon Humphrey, Congressman Robert Dornan and others.

Pat Robertson, who started the Christian Broadcasting Network (CBN) in 1960, which today reaches millions of TV viewers, urges Christians to get into the political arena so we can "place this nation under God."

"We have together," says Robertson, "with the Protestants and the Catholics, enough votes to run the country. And when the people say, 'We've had enough,' we are going to take over."

The Dallas Freedom Rally of Rev. James Robison in June 1979 showed that Christian people are ready. More than 12,000 people attended to protest against WFAA-TV Dallas, which threw evangelist Robison off the air in March because he preached against homosexuality.

The station claimed that Dr. Robison's sermon violated the Federal Communications Commission's Fairness Doctrine. A galaxy of religious and political stars spoke at the rally, including New Right leaders Howard Phillips and Paul Weyrich, who urged Christians to get more involved in politics.

Rev. Charles Stanley, pastor of the First Baptist Church of Atlanta, has reached over one million Americans with a videotape of his brilliant sermon, "Stand Up America," which calls on Christians to become active in politics.

Beyond question, Christians have already made their political presence felt.

- The IRS has abandoned, at least for the time being, its anti-church school campaign, primarily because Dr. Bob Billings, a New Right leader, organized a campaign that caused about 200,000 letters to be received by the IRS protesting their plans. At least another 200,000 letters and cards of protest were received by Jimmy Carter in the White House and Members of Congress.

- Rev. Robison's Freedom Rally raised $100,000 for legal expenses which were used successfully to force WFAA to put James Robison back on the air.

- Several states have passed laws protecting the independence of church schools.

In Indiana it was the Church Freedom Legislative Package. The man behind the legislation was Greg Dixon, pastor of the 8,000 member Indianapolis Baptist Temple. This legislative package removed control of parochial and private schools from the state. It also allowed churches to have unlicensed day care centers.

Virginia recently passed a law denying the state jurisdiction over Christian day care centers. The North Carolina legislature has limited the state's authority over church schools to health and safety, leaving classes and teacher credentials in the hands of the schools.

I believe these victories will multiply as Bible-believing Americans get better and better organized. And they are.

Jerry Falwell, for example, has formed the Moral Majority, Inc., an organization that aims to mobilize millions of Americans to work for pro-God, pro-family policies in government.

The Moral Majority claims it registered 2.5 million new voters and re-registered 1 to 1.5 million voters for the 1980 elections.

The Moral Majority has two arms—one for lobbying, one for education. The Moral Majority's executive director is Dr. Ron Godwin, who has lobbied for years for Christian causes in the nation's capitol.

The Moral Majority won't directly help candidates, but it will give politically concerned Christians a way to meet and work with each other.

And conservative Christians can be very effective in a political campaign—as the election of 1980 proved once and for all.

Despite some efforts to belittle it, the Moral Majority lived up to its publicity. It and allied groups gave Ronald Reagan his margin of victory.

Here is the way the ABC News-Lou Harris survey puts it:

"Ronald Reagan won his stunning victory last week not because the country as a whole went conservative, but because the conservatives—particularly the white moral majority—gave him such massive support.

"Among the 39% of the electorate that views itself as conservative in its political philosophy, Reagan won by an overwhelming 62-30% margin. This means that the conservatives gave him more than a 12 percentage point overall lead, before the votes of the rest of the electorate were counted. . . .

"However, a key segment of the conservative vote can be found among the 28% of the white voters who are followers of the so-called moral majority TV preachers. These organized groups with church affiliations were particularly active in this election. Most dramatically, it was their efforts which largely turned around the white Baptist vote in the South. Jimmy Carter won the white Baptist vote in 1976 by 56 to 43% against Gerald Ford. This time, he lost the white Baptists by a 56 to 34% margin. The white followers of the TV evangelical preachers gave Ronald Reagan two thirds of his 10 point margin in the election."

When New Right leader Donald E. (Buz) Lukens was first elected to Congress from Ohio in 1966, he had strong support from fundamentalist Christians. They made excellent workers because, as Lukens explains, they took their campaign commitment as a solemn personal responsibility. Buz also recalls that the endorsements he received from fundamentalist pastors were as stirring as any he has ever heard.

The foundation of the Moral Majority is fundamentalist Protestants, in particular the estimated 15 million Americans who watch Falwell's "Old Time Gospel Hour" regularly. Rev. Falwell has a remarkable base to work with. He already has 2 million names on his "Gospel Hour" mailing list.

But Dr. Falwell intends to build a coalition of not only his own religious followers but of Catholics, Jews and Mormons. Significantly, New Right leaders Paul Weyrich, an Eastern Rite Catholic, and Howard Phillips, a Jew, worked closely with Falwell in setting up the Moral Majority.

The potential of such a coalition is tremendous. There are an estimated 85 million Americans—50 million born-again Protestants, 30 million morally conservative Catholics, 3 million Mormons and 2 million Orthodox and Conservative Jews—with whom to build a pro-family, Bible-believing coalition.

Church leaders acknowledge that overcoming age-old suspicions among Catholics, Protestants and Jews won't be easy. But increasing threats from big government and big business (like mass media fascination with exploiting sex) make coming together an absolute necessity.

Another new political group is Christian Voice, whose board includes New Right Senators Orrin Hatch, James McClure and Roger Jepsen. The Los Angeles-based organization enlisted 37,000 clergymen from 45 denominations. It has more than 187,000 members and an annual budget of $3 million.

The group, headed by Rev. Robert Grant, was active in both the Rhodesia and Taiwan fights. Its expected opposition to liberalized homosexual rights prompted Gay Rights National Lobby representative Steve Endean to admit: "This is probably the most significant threat to gay progress on issues before the Congress that we've faced."

The chairman of Christian Voice, was one of the founders of American Christian Cause, which worked in Anita Bryant's Florida campaign and the California Briggs amendment efforts to limit homosexual influence.

In late September 1979, another major new conservative Christian organization was launched—The Religious Roundtable.

Founded by Ed McAteer, a businessman and lifelong Christian lay leader, Religious Roundtable meets four times a year for two days. Each two-day meeting will bring together 150 or more major Christian leaders. They discuss which national, political and governmental issues they should alert their millions of followers to take action on when they return home.

I can think of no better example to describe the New Right. It is talented, aggressive leaders meeting and deciding on a course of action in an important area. The Religious Roundtable is just one example of the type of coordinated, structured, conservative activity in a New Right area that didn't happen six years ago.

Through such leaders, the Roundtable aims to reach and activate tens of millions of other religious conservatives who will play a part when Congress considers legislation affecting abortion, private schools, prayer in schools, sex in the media and a strong national defense.

The first two-day session of the Religious Roundtable in September 1979 included remarks by Senator Gordon Humphrey, Phyllis Schlafly and New Right leaders Howard Phillips, Paul Weyrich, Richard Dingman of the House Republican Study Committee and myself on practical politics. Also speaking were Houston pollster Lance Tarrance on the political opinions of Americans of various religious denominations and Clay Claiborne, director of the Black Silent Majority.

Some of the other religious leaders who attended the first meeting of the Religious Roundtable were:

• Dr. Bob Billings, then executive director of Jerry Falwell's The Moral Majority.

• Dr. G. Cameron Townsend, founder of the Wycliffe Bible translators, with more than 15,000 missionaries in some 150 countries.

• Dr. Adrian Rogers, then president of the Southern Baptist Convention (1979-80), which represents 38,000 churches and 13 million Southern Baptists.

• Bob Dugan, director of public affairs for the National Association of Evangelicals, representing 35,000 churches of various denominations.

- John Talcott, founder and president of the Plymouth Rock Foundation, which prepares material for church school programs.

- Dr. Ben Armstrong, executive director of National Religious Broadcasting, representing 810 radio stations.

- John D. Beckett, president of Intercessors for America, a nationwide prayer organization.

- Bobby Richardson, former New York Yankees All-Star second basemen and popular banquet speaker for Christian causes.

There are many more Christian groups active across the country which can and should be mentioned.

The Cleveland law firm of Gibbs and Craze devotes five full-time lawyers to protecting Christian schools, foster homes and day care centers from bureaucratic assaults.

Pro-life groups of course depend heavily upon Catholics and conservative Protestants.

But there are others. Anita Bryant's campaign drew most of its members from Bible-believing Christians and Jews.

Mike Thompson, of Miami, Florida, who was communications director for the Bryant campaign, says flatly, "We put a new majority together in Dade County. We had the involvement of a total cross section of the community: Democrats, Republicans, Independents, all with the denominator of social conservatism."

Phyllis Schlafly's Stop-ERA and Eagle Forum have received strong support among church groups. When Schlafly and her allies organized the 1977 pro-family rally in Houston to counter Bella Abzug's women's lib conference, Christian churches across America bused in many of the 20,000 people who attended.

Mormons are prominent in two newer pro-family groups—Pro-Family United, an educational organization, and United Families of America, a lobbying group. The Mormon Church, by opposing ERA and abortion, has encouraged countless Mormons to get involved in these two battles. Phyllis Schlafly readily admits that Mormons gave her Stop-ERA forces the margin of victory in Florida, Nevada and Virginia.

Across the country, conservative preachers are beginning to lead and speak out on politics just as liberals like Protestants Rev. Andrew Young, Rev. Jesse Jackson, Rev. William Sloane Coffin, Rev. Martin Luther King, Jr. and Catholics Rev. Theodore Hesburgh and Father Robert Drinan have done.

During the 25 years that I've been active in politics, most of the major religious leaders in America have been liberals who were in the forefront of almost every liberal political cause—civil rights battles, Vietnam war rallies, reduction in military spending, and expansion of welfare.

For example, the ultra-liberal National Council of Churches:

• Advocated the admission of Red China to the United Nations as early as 1958.

• Came out against prayer in the public schools in 1963.

• Spoke out against the war in Vietnam in 1965.

• Pushed for a guaranteed annual income.

• Pressed for more foreign aid year after year.

Liberals are now complaining about conservative ministers who are just doing what liberal ministers have been doing for decades.

Conservative ministers have just been unable to sit back and accept the ultra-liberal actions of the World Council of Churches and projects like its so-called Program to Combat Racism.

The World Council shocked Christians around the World in August 1978 when it donated $85,000 to the pro-Marxist Patriotic Front of Zimbabwe (Rhodesia). The grant came shortly after the Patriotic Front boasted that it had shot down an unarmed Air Rhodesia airliner carrying civilians. The Front then denied it had any part in the massacre of the passengers who survived the crash.

According to the *New Republic*, the donation to the Patriotic Front ignited "a firestorm of protest" from Protestant clergy and laymen, revealing the gulf between the World Council and its constituency.

Christian Century, a liberal ecumenist magazine, described those who made the grant as "armchair guerrillas, vicarious doers of violence."

The Presbyterian Lay Committee, composed of members of United Presbyterian churches, accused the WCC of "subsidizing murderers" and urged the church to sever its ties with the world organization.

Catholics have been aroused by the continuing smear attacks on them because of their pro-life, anti-abortion stance. For example, Eleanor Smeal, president of the National Organization of Women (NOW), sent out a 1977 fund-raising letter which linked American Nazis, John Birch Society members, Ku Klux Klanners, and Roman Catholic bishops.

Smeal charged: "The intimidation of state and national legislators by the Roman Catholic hierarchy is an exercise of political power that threatens the rights of all Americans."

That is nonsense. The Catholic bishops do take positions on matters like abortion—but speaking out firmly is not intimidation.

Conservative Christians are also taking to the political barricades because of pornography—not just at the newsstands and TV and movies but in the public schools.

You may remember the textbook controversy in Kanawha County, West Virginia, in 1975. Liberals tried to picture the protestors as a bunch of ignorant rednecks out to burn books. But what upset Mrs. Alice Moore and other conservative parents were passages like the following from *Blue Denim*, a play to be read aloud by 12-and 13-year olds:

"Ernie: At first he thought he'd get four other guys to swear she's put out to *them* too, but then he decided he'd better do the honorable thing and get her an abortion."

And then there is television, the mass medium whose primary yardstick is, Does it sell? Apparently, sex sells very well.

Rev. Don Wildmon, founder of the National Federation for Decency, has reported:

• In the fall of the 1977, 1978 and 1979 seasons, almost 90% of all sex on TV was outside of marriage.

• During an average year of prime-time viewing, the TV audience is exposed to 11,531 sexually suggestive comments or scenes of implied sexual intercourse. If "skin scenes" (undue and unnecessary emphasis on the female anatomy) are added, the total rises to 18,429.

- During the 1979 monitoring period, the amount of profanity on the networks increased by 45.47% over a comparable 1978 period. A clear trend toward "hard profanity" is evident.

Don't say there's nothing you can do about it.

Rev. Don Wildmon has led several successful boycotts against advertisers on immoral programs.

In 1979, Rev. Wildmon headed a national boycott of Kentucky Fried Chicken because the company's owner, Heublein Corp., was sponsoring so much pornography on TV. As a result, Kentucky Fried Chicken is now limiting its advertising to news and children's programs.

The year before, he led a nationwide demonstration in 32 cities against Sears and Roebuck for its sponsorship of unwholesome TV programs. You know what? On the day of the demonstration, Sears withdrew its advertising from two of TV's most sexually provocative programs—"Three's Company" and "Charlie's Angels."

The Moral Majority has followed Rev. Wildmon's example with efforts to use economic boycotts to clean up TV. Already it has been accused of violating the Constitution for using the same weapon the Left has used with grapes, lettuce, wines, and Japanese-made goods—the only peaceful weapon available to the consumer of a medium that thrives by influencing consumer habits. As usual, the strident charges only mean that the Moral Majority has its opponents on the run.

The trend toward so-called "soft pornography" on TV must and can be stopped. If we don't act, the "porn" will get a little harder and a little more explicit each year.

That's what has happened with movies, books and magazines. A certain level of pornography is reached, and at first a majority of Americans are shocked and offended.

But after a while, people begin to feel they can't do anything about it. They accept what they see and hear. And the pornographers then reach for the next level.

That's the way the magazines went. First, there was *Esquire*, which in comparison with other "men's magazines" today seems as tame as *Jack and Jill*. Then came *Playboy*. Then *Penthouse*, then *Hustler* and a whole group of hardcore pornographic magazines which make a mockery of free speech.

Can this trend be stopped? Of course it can. And it can be done without violating the U.S. Constitution. The First Amendment was not designed to protect pornographers.

In the final analysis, it's up to each and every one of us.

Each American shares the responsibility to make America great again. We must use whatever talents God has given us.

This can take many directions. Community work, church activity and political involvement are just a few.

However, there are two things all of us can and should do which are more important than any other actions we could undertake. These are prayer and fasting.

I wrote in *Conservative Digest* in May/June, 1980 about the need for Americans to fast and ask God for forgiveness of our sins, ask for His protection, and give thanks for His blessings.

I proposed a National Day of Prayer and Fasting.

I urged Americans to petition Congress to proclaim the Sunday before Thanksgiving as a National Day of Prayer and Fasting.

I suggested this particular day because this is traditionally a time when Americans give thanks to God for all the blessings that we enjoy.

It would be a true and appropriate commemoration of the Thanksgiving season. And I feel it would make the spirit of Thanksgiving more meaningful to us.

George Washington set aside a day of fasting and prayer when he was President.

Also Abraham Lincoln, twice during the storm of our tragic Civil War, designated "a Sunday for prayer and fasting."

Twice during some of the darkest days of the American Revolutionary War, the Continental Congress declared a day of Fasting and Repentance.

Indeed, even Christ, when He knew He was soon to be tempted by the devil, prayed and fasted for 40 days.

The Bible tells us that bread cast upon water will return. And that you reap what you sow. I believe this is true for nations as well as individuals.

America was founded upon a belief in God. Our motto, "In God We Trust," reflects that belief. And as long as America held fast to that belief, God blessed us. About 16 years ago, America's problems seemed to significantly increase.

Civil unrest, racial strife, a lost war in Vietnam, illegal drug use, soaring inflation, a declining business climate, attacks on the family, sex and pornography in the movies and on TV, a lack of presidential leadership, a weak U.S. military and a strong and aggressive Soviet military are some examples of our major problems.

Today, world and national events look grim.

But as we look to the future, we shouldn't do so with worry and pessimism.

We worry when we see the Communists gaining military strength daily, and when a U.S. President seemed uninterested in opposing the Communist conquest of country after country.

But instead of worrying, why don't we as individuals and as a nation go to God and ask forgiveness for our sins?

Instead of worrying, why don't we pray that He protect America from its enemies and give us the strength and will to protect ourselves?

Why don't we thank God for the benefits He has bestowed on us as individuals and as a nation?

Perhaps many of our personal and national problems have developed because we have forgotten to thank God for our blessings, our opportunities, our freedoms and our great country.

The power of millions of Americans praying together for a common goal can have a profound effect.

By the way, I believe that those who want to play a leadership role in saving America and bringing freedom to the world should set aside not just one day a year, but one or more days a month exclusively devoted to prayer, fasting and meditation.

I believe that if we do, miracles will come to pass in our lives and in our country.

Remember, we are trying to take power away from those who govern this country and the world. And they are not going to give it up without a very, very tough, hard fight.

And we're not going to succeed without God's help.

Please include the men and women who are leading the fight for freedom in this country in your daily prayers.

XII

The Tax Revolt

For about 150 years in our history, until the late 1920's, total government spending stayed almost the same—about 10% of national income. And as late as 1925, personal income taxes remained quite low—from a minimum of about 1% to a maximum of 24%.

However, since the election of Franklin D. Roosevelt in 1932 and the liberal takeover of the nation's capital, government spending and government taxes have exploded.

So much so that today, Americans appear ready to fight against taxes and spending in a national rebellion from California to Washington, D.C.

According to Nobel economist Milton Friedman, "Total government spending—state, federal and local—(now) amounts to 40% of the national income."

In 1979, reports Don Lambro in his book *Fat City*, a typical taxpayer with a wife and two children earning $18,000 a year paid an "astounding $4,814 in federal taxes, including income, social security, excise and other levies."

The lion's share of personal income taxes, journalists Sheldon Engelmayer and Robert Wagman report, is paid by people having incomes between $17,000 and $40,000. Once your incomes goes over $17,000, you are in the top 50% of earners in America, and the top 50% pays 92% of all taxes, according to the IRS.

It took the federal government 175 years for its annual budget to reach $100 billion. It then took only nine years, from 1962 to 1971, for the federal budget to pass the $200 billion mark. It took another four years to hit $300 billion and just another two years to go over $400 billion.

By 1979, the federal government was spending almost $500 billion a year and reaching for $550 billion. The 1981 budget is expected to top $662.7 billion—easily.

At the same time, the government has consistently been spending more than it has taken in—running up deficits in 25 of the last 30 years. And it has had to borrow heavily to make up the difference. The 1980 deficit is expected to top $60 billion, with the government's total debt to reach (are you ready?) $859.2 billion.

Federal budget planners, says Lambro, have predicted that the total federal debt will be $951.9 billion, by 1982—almost *one trillion dollars.* The interest payments alone were about $57 billion in 1980.

This kind of irresponsible deficit spending by liberals has produced double-digit inflation, crushing taxes, soaring unemployment, and an aroused American public.

As Howard Jarvis might put it, "We're mad as hell and we're not going to take this anymore!"

The overwhelming passage of Proposition 13 in California in 1978, severely limiting property taxes, was felt across the country.

• Jeff Bell, a 30-year-old political scientist who never ran before for public office, beat New Jersey's four-term U.S. Senator, liberal Clifford Case, in the GOP primary that year. Bell's main campaign theme: a call for a one-third cut in personal income taxes.

• In the spring of 1978, Tennessee voted to limit tax increases to the rate of growth of the state's economy—the first state ever to adopt a constitutional spending limitation.

• Since then, Hawaii, Texas, Michigan, Arizona, Washington and California have all placed various legal lids on their states' spending. Colorado is the only state where voters rejected a constitutional spending limit—in 1978.

• In 1980, Missouri, Alaska, and Massachusetts all passed significant tax limitation or reduction measures. And, of course, we elected a president pledged to the Kemp-Roth proposal to cut income taxes 30% over the next three years.

Tax cuts are not only good politics but good economics, too.

UCLA economist Arthur Laffer, a top advisor to Congressman Kemp, argues that taxes in America are so high they discourage companies from expanding and employees from trying to make more money. Laffer says that a tax cut would unleash new economic energies which would greatly expand the tax base. The result: the government would lose little in total tax receipts or actually take in more as lower tax rates generated more taxable income for all Americans.

Neo-conservative columnist Michael Novak puts it this way:

"For the first time in 40 years, the Republicans are in a position to offer more than Democrats: '*More* of your own money in your own pocket.'

" 'Keep it out of the hands of government,' the Republicans can now say. 'Keep *more* of it for yourself.' "

If we do not act, and soon, the United States could go the way of Great Britain.

Already, many of our factories and machines have become outmoded. Our industrial cities have run down. Our work force has become less productive.

Real growth has declined in the face of high taxes and crushing government regulation. In short, as *Time* magazine has commented, America "is losing its economic edge in the world, and the hour is late—very late."

Frankly, what we must do is stop socialism.

Thirty-two years ago, liberal philosopher Arthur Schlesinger, Jr., wrote in *Partisan Review* that he saw "no inherent obstacle to the gradual advance of socialism in the United States through a series of New Deals."

He was right. Our marvelous system of government, though created by patriots of great genius, does not adequately protect private citizens against the power of big government.

Local, state and national legislators have proved unable to resist the demands for more money by bureaucrats and the thousands of pleas by liberal do-gooders (and socialists) who insist on doing "good" with someone else's money.

"It is the first principle of politics where (Teddy) Kennedy comes from," columnist Joseph Sobran wrote, "that when you *care* about people, you show it by spending other people's money on them."

Even candidates who win election sincerely promising to cut spending and taxes, often collapse when the highly effective liberals apply pressure.

And, of course, some candidates try to fool the voters by saying anything to get elected. Once elected, a politician has the advantage of incumbency and can often win reelection even if he breaks his promise to fight big spending. Besides that, with our combination of inflation and the progressive tax rate, members of Congress can have their expanded government programs and never have to vote for a tax increase.

Fifteen years ago, Morton Blackwell asked Milton Friedman if the growth of government could be stopped. Yes, he replied, but only if that growth becomes so rapid and painful that citizens will rise up and fight to turn back the trend while there is still enough strength left in the private sector to resist the invasion of government.

The citizen's revolt is here and now. The tax-spend-elect system of Franklin D. Roosevelt is bearing the bitter fruit of inflation, recession and unemployment.

Our economy is suffering from the worst period of inflation since Alexander Hamilton stabilized the dollar almost 200 years ago.

Our government, at all levels, eats up about half of each dollar our free enterprise system produces.

Businessmen are so over-regulated and harassed by bureaucrats that they are losing what is left of economic freedom.

In the auto industry, *Newsweek* reported in March 1979, government fuel efficiency and safety standards over the past decade have added as much as $600 to the price of every car. Those air bags being promoted so aggressively by Ralph Nader would add another $500 to every auto.

140

OSHA's initial proposal to limit noise in the workplace would cost an estimated $10 billion. EPA's original plan to maintain what it considers an "acceptable" ozone level in the atmosphere could have run as high as $20 billion. Pollution control in 1980, according to *Newsweek*, would cost state and local governments as well as industry over $14 billion.

The statewide campaigns I have mentioned as well as hundreds of local efforts attest to the continuing strength of the national tax rebellion.

But state and local anti-tax victories aren't enough. If every state and every local government limited their taxes and balanced their budget, that would not halt the gradual advance of socialism at the most important level—the federal government.

Congress has shown again and again that it cannot discipline itself. We must, as Thomas Jefferson said, "bind them down with the chains of the Constitution."

The relentless growth of our federal government can be stopped. We can do it by amending our Constitution and plugging up the loopholes by which the federal government is gradually destroying our economic freedom and thereby all our freedoms.

There are two exciting proposals which together form what this country needs so badly—a firm and unyielding obstacle to socialism that Arthur Schlesinger, Jr., accurately saw did not exist 32 years ago.

First is the balanced budget proposal which is being shepherded by the National Taxpayers Union, headed by James Davidson. As of this writing, 29 state legislatures have petitioned the Congress to call a constitutional convention for a balanced budget amendment to our Constitution. When five more states join these 29, Congress must either call the convention or pass a balanced budget Constitutional amendment.

The second proposal is the spending limitation amendment being sponsored by the National Tax Limitation Committee, directed by Lewis Uhler, a former top Reagan aide in California who authored the historic state tax-limitation amendment, Proposition 1, in 1973. The NTLC amendment, largely the brainchild of Dr. Friedman, will be introduced in the 1981 session of Congress.

This amendment would reverse the trend of increasing tax bites and stop the process by which government gets a bigger cut of your income as inflation pushes you into higher tax brackets.

Both these proposals contain safeguards to permit higher spending in times of real national emergency, such as war or other national calamity.

We conservatives must strike while the iron is hot. If we are ever going to put a halt to big government, we must not let this chance slip through our fingers. We must channel the fierce public uproar over inflation and high taxes into effective action now.

It's going to be a hard fight. Most of the bureaucrats, big labor, big media, and the liberals and socialists will fight us tooth and nail against these two amendments.

They will try to talk them both to death. They will try to frighten voters just as California liberals tried to do prior to the passage of Proposition 13 in 1978. They failed then, but the liberals were successful in June 1980 in scaring the voters of California into voting against Proposition 9, which would have cut state income tax rates by half.

Our victories will not come easily. If there were an easy solution, we'd have stopped the growth of big government long ago. But this is a fight we can and *must* win for all Americans.

Both the balanced budget and the spending limitation amendments are good and needed. Together they will work an economic miracle in America.

We must make it as politically painful as possible for a U.S. Senator, Congressman or state legislator to oppose either amendment. Don't let any politicians wriggle off the hook by supporting only one of the amendments. America needs both.

Let your elected representatives know you're watching them like a hawk, waiting to see how hard they fight to pass these amendments. Don't let up on them until you win their active support for both.

And don't let your friends be fooled by liberal claims that these amendments are too restrictive, that the politicians need more "flexibility." Liberal flexibility has stopped our country's economic growth and produced a kind of rubber money that just won't stretch any more.

There is one other thing we must do and that is stop the waste in Washington. Don Lambro, one of UPI's finest investigative reporters, spent three years researching and writing *Fat City*, (Regnery/Gateway, Inc., 1980) which should be read by every taxpayer.

Lambro estimates that "at least $100 billion a year in taxes is unnecessarily going to the federal government to be squandered on programs our country could better do without."

Think of it—$100 billion a year, nearly one-sixth of the annual federal budget.

Here are just a few of the 100 federal programs proposed for the ax by Don Lambro as outlined by editor Marvin Stone of *U.S. News & World Report:*

• Community Services Administration, $668 million. The 800 local Community Action Programs supported in part by the CSA should exist with the consent of state and local elected officials rather than continue as costly, ineffective appendages of the federal bureaucracy.

• Youth Conservation Corps, $70 million. It aids mostly white, middle-class young people who are already employable and don't need government help.

• Government film-making, $500 million. Most of the films are "frivolous, self-promoting and duplicative." A few film titles will tell you all you need to know: "Your Teeth Are in Your Hands" (a $35,000 film series made by the Navy to instruct recruits on how to care for their teeth); "Mulligan Stew" (a $300,000 film of the Agriculture Department, to teach children about good nutrition, a subject already taught in every school system in America); "America on the Rocks" (a $375,000 film by HEW, which discovered that alcoholism is a middle-class problem).

The National Endowment for the Arts reached a new low by underwriting one-third of the cost of a 30-minute film showing a dog being shot to death again and again.

• The U.S. Travel Service, $8 million. It duplicates work done better by non-government organizations.

• The Small Business Administration, $1.5 billion. An agency, in the words of Marvin Stone, "full of mismanagement, political favoritism and outright fraud."

• The Alaska Railroad, $8 million. The government should sell the railroad to private enterprise or turn it over to the state of Alaska.

143

- Highway Beautification Program, $20.5 million. State control programs and local community sign laws are adequate enough to deal with any billboard problem.

- The Federal Election Commission, $8.5 million. The FEC, Lambro wrote, "has heaped bureaucratic supervision and harassment and censorship upon our most fundamental . . . right."

- Federal Trade Commission, $65 million. The FTC, says Lambro, "is a supremely unnecessary and wasteful federal agency that the nation can no longer afford."

- Council on Wage and Price Stability, $5.9 million. "The place to start cutting the federal budget," argues Lambro, "would be to abolish this agency."

Please note that none of the above or any of the programs listed in *Fat City* would seriously threaten services and benefits for the poor, the sick, the elderly, the disabled, the jobless.

Lambro declares, "Government can be significantly reduced in size, and not a single truly needy American has to be denied benefits and services he or she truly deserves."

In fact, the reductions proposed in *Fat City* would provide more for the disadvantaged just as Ronald Reagan's welfare reform in California resulted in increased benfits for those truly in need.

And of course the elimination of wasteful programs would mean a reduction in the taxes needed for such programs, enabling Americans to better care for themselves.

In addition to wasteful programs which ought to be eliminated, Don Lambro describes wasteful practices which our federal government ought to stop without delay. Here are some of the more flagrant examples:

- The government loses more than $500 million a year in bad debts—such as from small business loans or Veterans Administration overpayments—which are routinely written of as "uncollectible."

The Department of Education admitted in July 1980 that 875,000 former students have defaulted on government education loans totalling $731.7 million, a default rate of 16%.

- White-collar cheaters and swindlers are reaping an estimated $15 billion (according to the Government Accounting Office) from federal economic assistance programs.

- Nearly 4,000 audit reports "are gathering dust on government shelves," although they document the loss of $4.3 billion annually in unauthorized use of federal funds by contractors and grant recipients.

- Federal employees now spend nearly $8 billion a year on travel—much of it first class. In 1976, the Small Business Administration (4,300 employees) spent $4.7 million on travel—over $1,000 for every secretary, billing clerk and manager.

Economist Thomas Sowell of UCLA has summed up federal poverty programs:

"To be blunt, the poor are a gold mine. By the time they are studied, advised, experimented with, and administered, the poor have helped many a middle-class liberal to achieve affluence with government money."

Writing in the *New York Times Magazine*, Sowell said, "The total amount of money the government spends on its many antipoverty efforts is three times what would be required to lift every man, woman and child in America above the official poverty line by simply sending money to the poor."

Yes, as always, it is the poor who suffer the most from inflation, from taxation, from regulation, from liberalism.

Inflation makes the poor poorer. Taxes push up prices. Laws like the minimum wage prevent the poor from getting jobs. And liberalism offers the poor a handout while placing its foot on their neck.

The wealthy do most of the complaining, as J. Kenser Kahn says, but have the wealth to avoid real suffering. The middle class loses the most. But the poor who already do not have enough for their needs suffer the most from inflation and taxes because they must get along on even less.

New Right leader Howard Phillips, chosen by Nixon in 1973 to undertake the dismantling of the Office of Economic Opportunity, recalls: "I visited health programs where the main concern was registering voters. . . . 81% of OEO's funds went in one form or another to overhead costs."

145

• The federal government is spending more than $1.5 billion every year "to promote, communicate and sell" its programs and accomplishments to the American people. There is now an army of nearly 20,000 "public relations" specialists in the various federal departments and agencies. The $1.5 billion includes the previously mentioned $500 million for audio-visual programs, more than $200 million for advertising and about $400 million for all other PR and public information programs, including the salaries of that 20,000 person federal "army."

• The Department of Labor's job-training program (CETA) is riddled with waste and mismanagement. In Nashville, Tenn., $12,000 was spent in 1979 to teach adults to "groom properly and use the telephone effectively." CETA is financing a body-building course for Pittsburgh women who want to work in the steel mills.

• In 1978, the Labor Department gave Cesar Chavez $500,000 to teach English to members of his militant ultra-liberal United Farm Workers.

• American business annually spends $32 billion, reports Lambro, to comply with the paperwork demands of Washington. It costs individuals, that is, you and me, nearly $9 billion a year to meet their paperwork requirements, mostly tax forms. The federal government spends more than $43 billion to print, process, compile and store federal forms. Lambro estimates that at least $100 billion "is sucked from our economy to comply with this paperwork passion."

The Environmental Protection Agency reduced one of its forms to one page—but you had to read a 90-page introduction of instructions to fill it out.

Then there is OSHA—the Occupational Safety and Health Administration—"Washington's most hated agency," to use Lambro's phrase.

Since 1970, when it was created, OSHA has been responsible for overseeing 6 million American businesses having one or more employees. The result has not been an improvement in health and safety among American businesses but deepening anger, resentment and contempt of OSHA.

It's easy to understand why when you consider the sheer stupidity of many of OSHA's demands:

— An OSHA inspector told a Florida meat-packing company a safety railing had to be put around its loading dock to keep workers from falling off. After the company put up the railing, an Agriculture Department inspector ordered it removed as an obstacle to sanitation.

— A Massachusetts supermarket was ordered to install a nonslip grating on its workspace floor. Along came Agriculture again, and the market was forced to rip out the grating and install a sanitary tile floor. Cost to the store (and ultimately to the store's customers): $25,000.

— The University of Illinois was forced to spend $557,000 when OSHA ruled that railings along an elevated walkway connecting campus buildings were a few inches too short. OSHA required all such railings be exactly 42 inches high.

Some American businessmen have fought back, most notably Ferrol G. (Bill) Barlow of Pocatello, Idaho.

In September 1975, an OSHA inspector, unexpected and unannounced, walked into Barlow's small heating and plumbing shop. Barlow politely refused him admission, citing the Fourth Amendment as protecting him "against unreasonable searches." Barlow said he would be happy to comply *if* the OSHA agent could produce a search warrant that provided a probable cause for OSHA to believe that some violation existed in the Barlow shop.

A legal battle followed, all the way to the U.S. District Court in Idaho, where a three-judge panel ruled in Barlow's favor, and finally to the U.S. Supreme Court, which agreed that OSHA must produce a search warrant if the employer demands it. It was a satisfying but expensive victory, with legal costs for Barlow of more than $100,000.

• The National Science Foundation has a passion for spending taxpayers' money on sex-related research projects. They have included a $121,000 grant to determine the effect of marijuana on men's ability to become sexually aroused. The NSF has also given away $40,000 on a study of the origins of Polynesian culture, $200,000 on the speech patterns of the people of Philadelphia, $22,000 on polygamy among birds, $24,000 on the reproductive strategies of milkweeds, and $81,300 on the sociosexual behavior of the dabbing African black duck.

• Since the Department of Housing and Urban Development (HUD) was established in 1965, it has spent more than $76 billion to provide decent housing for Americans. The result, in Lambro's words, "has been an enormous $76 billion disappointment." Millions of Americans still live in substandard urban and rural housing.

According to the government, federal housing programs have financed the construction of more than 1 million housing units. Yet with HUD's $76 billion, Lambro points out, the government "could have bought—at today's inflated prices—more than 1.5 million new $50,000 single-family homes."

What went wrong was summed up by *Washington Post* reporter Jackson Diehl in a 1979 article, entitled "Ghostly Remains":

"Billions of tax dollars were spent nationally—and millons were poured into the Pumpkin Hill apartments (in South Laurel, Maryland)—in pursuit of this Kennedy-Johnson dream of decent, affordable housing for every American.

"What millions of tax dollars bought in the case of Pumpkin Hill are apartments that Prince George's County Executive Lawrence J. Hogan recently called, 'threats to human life.'

"Pumpkin Hill, moreover, is one of six federally subsidized housing fiascoes in Prince George's County. Almost $35 million—five times the amount the government set out to spend—has been poured into the Pumpkin Hill, Central Gardens, Washington Heights, Baber Village, Nalley and Glenarden apartment projects.

"What HUD has to show for that $35 million today are six ugly and dangerous suburban slums.

"The big losers—besides the taxpayers—are the very people that the 2,140 apartment units were built to help."

Diehl's story, according to Lambro, "has been written in most major cities in the country." The greatest tragedy of all, he adds, is that:

"Instead of the poor, it is the banks, private developers, investors, consultants, contractors, and their own employees who have been among HUD's most successful beneficiaries."

The same could be said of federal program after federal program.

I could go on and on giving you more and more horror stories, but I'm sure the point of how Washington wastes our taxes has been made.

I now think, and hope, that I'm going to shock you by saying, you and I are basically responsible for Fat City. And it is up to you and to me to change it.

You and I have allowed politicians and bureaucrats to use *our* government and *our* tax dollars for their special greedy ends. But we can stop them if we choose to.

The balanced budget and spending limitation amendments are excellent ideas. Similar limits could be placed on state governments as well. In addition, we could require, by statute or amendment, that 4% of the Federal budget *each year* be set aside for repayment of the federal debt.

Finally, we can amend the Constitution, if necessary, to place a limit on the federal income tax rate. Milton Friedman has estimated that an across the board tax rate of less than 20%—with no deductions except for strict job expenses—would produce *more* federal revenues than the present system.

As Congressman Phil Crane has said, referring to the religious custom of tithing, "If God asks for 10%, Caesar should ask for no more."

There are countless other measures that can and should be taken against government waste of public and private resources. But once we have set stern limits on what Washington can do to us as taxpayers, we will automatically reduce the overregulation and self-indulgent fringe benefits with which the federal government has burdened us. The same is true of the states.

The main thing is to protect those who actually produce our nation's wealth: the taxpayers. A long step in that direction would be the adoption of Senator Jesse Helms's "Taxpayers' Bill of Rights Act," which would do the following:

• Require IRS agents to inform the taxpayer of his right to counsel and his right to remain silent.

• Provide for the government to pay attorney's fees in cases won by the taxpayer.

- Set up an Assistant Commissioner for Taxpayer Services to act as an ombudsman within the IRS for the people.

- Authorize the GAO to audit regularly the efficiency and fairness of the IRS.

XIII

The Pro-Family Movement

Today, many liberals are declaring that the traditional family is dead. Well, there are lots of available statistics that suggest that while not dead, the American family is far from healthy.

• Nearly 1 out of every 2 marriages now ends in divorce.

• Nationally, one out of every five births is illegitimate. In 1978, there were more illegitimate than legitimate births in both New York City and Washington, D.C.

• There were an estimated 12 million cases of venereal disease among young people in 1979, according to the U.S. Surgeon General.

• There have been an estimated 1 million abortions a year in America since the Supreme Court decision of January 1973.

• Six out of 10 married women with school-age children work.

• In Los Angeles alone, 30,000 children are being exploited for pornographic books, magazines, films and prostitution.

At the 1978 convention of the National Right to Life Committee, Dr. Harold Voth, a senior psychiatrist at the Menninger Foundation, declared that the fundamental unit of every society is the family which, in his professional opinion, is deteriorating in modern America.

American pioneers were strong, God-fearing and family-oriented. They built houses and families to last. They lived, worked and died together.

But, said Dr. Voth, industrialization, wars, economic pressures and working mothers have all combined to deprive children of good parenting. And without good committed parents, there can be few healthy children. And without healthy children, a society soon loses its vitality.

There is an urgent need, the Menninger psychiatrist argued, to make the family flourish again, to fight anti-family organizations like the National Organization of Women and to resist laws like the Equal Rights Amendment that attack families and individuals.

"Strong families and strong leaders built this country," said Dr. Voth, "and strong families and strong leaders will save it."

Which is what the pro-family movement aims to do. Paul Weyrich, a leader of the New Right and of this new pro-family coalition, believes that family issues in the 1980s could be what Vietnam was in the 1960s and environmental and consumer issues were in the 1970s for the Left.

Millions of Americans have been politically awakened by such issues as:

• May our children pray at school?

• Should children be flooded with pornography?

• Should wives and mothers be drafted into our armed forces?

• Should abortions be encouraged by the federal government?

• Should the federal government regulate relations between husband and wife, between parent and child?

The pro-family movement is an incredibly dynamic coalition of groups—many of which didn't exist two years ago, and most of whose members are getting into politics for the first time.

The pro-family movement has enormous political strength—in its outreach and in its moral commitment. As Paul Weyrich says, "As pro-family groups become better educated in the political process, a lot of Congressmen who today thumb their noses at the whole notion of a pro-family coalition are going to be humbled."

Because so many anti-family laws and regulations flow from Washington, D.C., pro-family leaders set up an organization in the nation's capital in the summer of 1979. They call themselves "Library Court," after the tiny street on Capitol Hill where the original meeting place was located. The coalition represents more than 20 national groups.

They have gotten off to a fast start. In 1979, the Library Court group sponsored a flood of letters to the Department of Health, Education and Welfare protesting its plans for test-tube baby research. Their campaign forced HEW to put the project on the back burner.

In 1980, the group has fought both the Domestic Violence Bill—an unwarranted federal intrusion into family matters—and Sen. Edward Kennedy's Criminal Code Recodification Bill, which would enact ERA through the back door, weaken federal controls over pornography and legitimize homosexuality.

They are already a political force to be reckoned with.

Dr. William Gribbin, social policy analyst for the Senate Republican Policy Committee, says: "The organized pro-family effort, as manifested by Library Court meetings, has already made a major impact on the legislative process during the 96th Congress, and that impact is likely to grow in the future."

Members of Library Court are quick to emphasize that their first commitment is to traditional pro-family, pro-God values. They are political conservatives second, and sometimes not at all.

Jim Wright, chairman of the Maryland-based Christian Coalition for Legislative Action and one of Library Court's most active members, says that "the pro-family movement is not a subset of the conservative movement."

The pro-family movement is made up of people of many faiths—Catholic, Protestant, Jewish, Eastern Orthodox.

Paul Weyrich is very optimistic about the future impact of the pro-family movement. "In sheer numbers," he asserts, "the potential outreach of the Library Court group is greater than the whole range of conservative groups."

The chairman of Library Court is Mrs. Connaught (Connie) Marshner, director of the Family Policy Division of the Free Congress Foundation, and a tireless writer, speaker and debater. For example, in the first half of 1980, she spoke in a dozen states, appeared on such national talk shows as *The 700 Club*, and conducted an average of six interviews a week with major newspapers and magazines. Connie's book, *Blackboard Tyranny*, has become gospel for the education groups in the pro-family movement.

Some other members of Library Court include: Bob Baldwin, executive director, Citizens for Educational Freedom; Judie Brown, president, American Life Lobby; William Chasey, executive vice president for governmental and political affairs, the Religious Roundtable; Jack Clayton, Washington representative, American Association of Christian Schools; Sharon Pelton, social issues director, Conservatives Against Liberal Legislation; Susan Phillips, director of research and publications, The Conservative Caucus Research, Analysis and Education Foundation; Louise Ropog, administrative assistant, Family America; Kathy Teague, executive director, American Legislative Exchange Council, and Jim Wright, chairman, Christian Coalition for Legislative Action.

While the pro-family movement, like many New Right efforts, spends much of its time fighting liberal measures, it is also leading the campaign for a major new piece of legislation which would make wholesome family life a national priority.

The legislation is the Family Protection Act, introduced by Sen. Paul Laxalt of Nevada in September 1979. The Family Protection Act is a major project of the conservative movement. Connie Marshner worked closely with Senator Laxalt in drafting the bill.

The act will be a benchmark for years to come for the kind of sensible actions the federal government should be taking to preserve traditional family values in America.

It reasserts the rights of parents in rearing and educating their children. It seeks to protect the rights of private schools. It gives parents a greater role in textbook review. It denies government favoritism for homosexuality.

In short, the bill attempts to reestablish the family as the basic unit of strength for America.

After introducing the Family Protection Act, Senator Laxalt hosted a luncheon for a group of the nation's top evangelical leaders who promised an all-out effort to pass the bill. Senator Laxalt said that "for years we have been debating on the terms of those who want to remake society. Now those groups will have to explain why they oppose the traditional idea of the family."

The legislation contains several unique tax ideas such as: a tax incentive for Americans to provide same-home care for their own parents; IRA (Individual Retirement Account) -type savings accounts which would enable parents to save money for the education of their children; IRA's for spouses; and repeal of the inequities of the marriage tax.

The Family Protection Act is a detailed piece of legislation running over 50 pages. Here are some of its provisions:

• Federal education money shall be denied states that forbid prayer in public buildings.

• No federal money shall be used to buy textbooks that belittle the traditional role of women in society.

• A household which includes a dependent person over 65 may claim a $1000 tax exemption.

• No college student shall receive food stamps.

• An employed person may contribute up to $1500, tax deductible, to a savings account for a non-working spouse.

Some conservative may ask, "Is such a far-reaching piece of legislation really necessary? Doesn't it go against the conservative philosophy by trying to legislate morality and the American family?"

My quick and firm answer to the first question is, "Yes, the Family Protection Act is urgently needed because of all the liberal anti-family legislation and other actions over the last two decades."

And my answer to the second question is, "No, the Family Protection Act is not anti-conservative because conservatives believe that 'he who pays the piper should call the tune.' If taxpayer funds are used their elected representatives ought to be able to determine how such funds shall be used."

Frankly, nothing shows more clearly the sharp difference between the New Right and what might be called the old right than the Family Protection Act.

In the past, conservatives concentrated almost always on resisting liberal anti-family actions.

In contrast, the Family Protection Act of Senator Paul Laxalt is an across-the-board, in depth omnibus bill which has already thrown the liberals off-balance and will significantly strengthen the American family.

How needed is the Family Protection Act? Let me give you just a few examples of what the liberals have done to our way of life since the early 1960s.

• In 1962 and 1963, the Supreme Court held that voluntary prayer or Bible reading in the public schools violated the U.S. Constitution.

• Lyndon Johnson's Elementary and Secondary Education Act of 1965 began, in the words of House Education and Labor Committee staffer Lawrence Uzzell, "a massive shift of decision making power" away from parents and local school boards to teacher unions and state and federal bureacracies."

• In the mid-1960s, sociologist James S. Coleman authored a massive study which was widely used to justify busing to bring about school desegregation.

• In March 1972, Congress sent the Equal Rights Amendment to the states by an overwhelming majority.

• The January 1973 decision of the Supreme Court made abortion on demand the law of the land.

• Throughout the 1970s, there was an increasing legal trend toward decriminalization of marijuana with a resulting increase in the use of all drugs, especially among young people. According to the U.S. Surgeon General, by 1976, 60% of the 18-25 year-old group had used marijuana. 20% had "graduated" to harder drugs.

• The creation of the Department of Education in 1979 further extends federal control over education.

Do we need the Laxalt Family Protection Act? You bet we do.

One of the latest attempts of the federal government to intrude itself into the affairs of the family is the proposed Domestic Violence Act.

There's no denying that violence within the family is on the rise. The FBI reports that in 1978, 19% of the 19,555 people murdered in the U.S. were killed by a family member. Half of these involved the killing of one spouse by another.

Domestic violence, as Sen. Orrin Hatch has commented, affects all families—urban and rural, rich and poor, civilian and military. The victims are usually women who need protection for themselves and their children.

The liberals, typically, have come up with a new totally federal answer to this serious problem—the Domestic Violence Prevention and Services Act. The bill would create an OSHA-type agency. It would make all state and local jurisdictions answerable to a new Washington bureaucracy—the Federal Interagency Council on Domestic Violence.

As Senator Hatch has said, "This bill is one giant step by the federal social service bureaucracy into family matters which are properly, effectively and democratically represented in the state and local communities."

I agree with the Senator that most Americans do not want this new bureaucracy. Most Americans want a reduction and not an increase in federal interference and control.

And then there is the 1980 White House Conference on Families—an event organized, as New Right leader JoAnn Gasper has said, to drum up support for more federal spending, more federal regulations, and more political power for "alternative lifestyle" groups like homosexuals and women's libbers.

When pro-family forces won delegate contests in Oklahoma, Minnesota, Virginia and Maryland in late 1979 and early 1980, the liberals panicked.

Many states which had planned to elect most of their delegates changed their plans so that most delegates were appointed by the governors rather than elected. The governors, influenced by state steering committees usually controlled by liberals, appointed mostly liberal delegates to the conference.

Two conservative governors, Democrat Fob James of Alabama and Republican Otis Bowen of Indiana, decided not to cooperate with Jimmy Carter's attempted propaganda boost for more government involvement in family matters. Both Gov. James and Gov. Bowen declined to send delegates from their states.

The liberals' rhetoric was disgraceful. Delegates who opposed the Conference's anti-family bias were called "radical," "extremists" and "bigots."

The worst fears of the pro-family forces were realized at the June 1980 eastern regional meeting of the White House Conference on Families in Baltimore when the mostly appointed delegates endorsed the "right" to abortion, the Equal Rights Amendment, nondiscrimination against homosexuals, national health insurance and a guaranteed annual income of $13,000 for a family of four.

Many of the Pro-Family Coalition, led by New Right leaders Connie Marshner and Virginia state legislator Larry Pratt, walked out of the Baltimore meeting in protest. They refused to be part of such a Big Brother approach to the problems of the American family. As did the Catholic bishops of America after first agreeing to participate.

Dr. V. Dallas Merrell, president of the United Families of America, has set forth what he and other New Right groups want from the federal government.

• American families do not want guaranteed annual incomes—they want lower taxes and relief from inflation.

• American families do not want more but fewer welfare programs and a corresponding reduction in government spending. Federal spending eats into the family's income, forcing mothers to go to work to pay for food, clothing, shelter and other family basics.

• American families do not want national health insurance which drives up the cost of hospitals and doctors (as Medicare and Medicaid have done), but tax incentives so that families can choose their own form of private health care.

In a statement given to the White House Conference on Families, Dr. Merrell stressed that his organization welcomed such innovations as "flextime," which permits mothers and fathers to better manage their time at home; increased use of computer terminals and telecommunications to allow more adults to work at home; recreational and educational opportunities at the neighborhood and community level rather than the citywide level.

Summed up Dr. Merrell:

"Government should get out of the way of the traditional family and should stop searching for 'alternatives' to it. We believe that the family is the basic unit of our society. As G.K. Chesterton said, 'As are families, so is society.' "

But as we've seen, it is almost impossible for liberals to keep their hands off any part of our society—including its basic unit, the family.

In the December 1979 issue of *Ms.* magazine, Gloria Steinem published what Paul Weyrich called, "a blueprint for destroying the family." Encouraged by the spread of abortion, homosexuality, ERA, drugs and other anti-family factors, Steinem wrote that "we are now ready for more institutional, systematic change in the 1980's."

The liberals, Paul says, plan to paint those who believe in traditional values "as a reactionary minority" trying to impose its outmoded ideas on the rest of society.

Well, we are *not* a reactionary minority but a traditional majority seeking to preserve American society as we have always known it.

However, I have to say I am disappointed to see so much of conservatives' energies spent on the "Thou Shalt Nots" of the Old Testament.

Of course I believe in the Thou Shalt Nots, but I also believe in the softness, gentleness and love of Christ. And I know that most all of my conservative friends do also, but many times the public doesn't see it.

For example, I share conservatives' disapproval of homosexuality. It is wrong and I want to do what I can to keep it from being considered as an acceptable alternative lifestyle.

But I would like to see conservatives show as great or even a greater interest in opposing pre-marital sex and adultery.

Pre-marital sex and adultery, in my view, are much more serious threats to our society than homosexuality. They lead to over half a million illegitimate births a year and the break up of millions of marriages and broken homes for tens of millions of children.

There's another crisis in the American family today—the failure of our public schools to teach basic skills.

Dan Alexander, president of the Mobile, Alabama, board of education and an upcoming New Right leader, decided in 1978 that one answer was competency tests for teachers. The results were dramatic and revealing; only about half of the Mobile applicants who took the competency test in 1979 passed.

Alexander started a national movement. Some form of teacher testing has been approved in 12 states. Proposals for teacher testing have been introduced or are pending in nine other states. Polls show that 85% of U.S. adults favor teacher testing.

Here are some other needed reforms:

• A tightening up of standards in the education programs at the 1,150 colleges that train teachers.

• An abandoning of education fads like the New Math, the "open classroom," and the look-say approach to reading (rather than the more effective "phonics" method).

• Better and more balanced textbooks. Norma Gabler of Longview, Texas, a New Right leader, has long been the nation's leading advocate of balanced textbooks for public schools. Because Texas is such a big market for textbook publishers, Mrs. Gabler has forced several textbook companies to rewrite their texts for the entire country.

• Eliminating bureaucratic regulations that require teachers to deal with public health officials, social workers, insurance companies, juvenile police, and even divorce lawyers (about child custody).

• Dealing more effectively with violence in schools. The Pennsylvania legislature, for example, is considering a bill that would make carrying a gun or knife in school a serious crime.

• Encouraging principals to be more decisive in managing their schools.

• Getting Parent-Teacher Associations to become more involved.

And most important of all:

• Understanding that teaching children to read and write and do sums correctly is not all that hard—unless you make it so.

Who and what is behind the anti-family movement? Weyrich lists the major ones as those who do not believe in God, hardcore socialists, economic opportunists eager to make a buck from pornography, abortion, etc., and women's libbers who want a different political and cultural order.

As far as the New Right and the entire pro-family movement are concerned, the lines have been drawn.

We will work in Washington, in state capitals, in cities and towns, in schools and churches, everywhere that is necessary, to protect and preserve the American family as it has developed and evolved during our country's 200 year history.

As columnist Joseph Sobran has written, "The last stronghold of private freedom is the family."

XIV

Blue Collars and Blacks

There are two groups whose support the liberals have long taken for granted. But in 1980, union members simply ignored their own leaders by the millions. And it may not be long before millions of blacks do the same.

For many years, blue collar workers were unquestioningly loyal to the union leadership—because that leadership was loyal to them. They could count on it to look after their interests, and not to run counter to the interests of America.

That's no longer true. And both sides know it.

The pattern is familiar: as with many groups, the unions' nominal leadership has lost touch with the rank-and-file. Union officials and the workers differ sharply on such issues as the Panama Canal, ERA, welfare, forced school busing, food stamps, and national defense. The union leaders also devote their concern—and the workers' dues—to trendy liberal causes the workers couldn't care less about, like the Department of Education.

George Wallace got enough votes in his presidential campaigns to prove that the American blue-collar worker is right of center and anti-Communist. Wallace was denounced by the union leadership.

A 1980 study by Dr. Dan C. Heldman and Deborah L. Knight revealed that union political action committees have heavily backed anti-defense candidates. Of the six large PACs they examined, all donated from 63% to 71% of their campaign funds to "anti-national security" candidates, and only 7% to 16% to "pro-national security" candidates.

Other studies back this up. A 1977 study by *The New Right Report*, found that 96% of the AFL-CIO's COPE contributions to challengers in 1976 was spent *against* incumbents who scored above 70% on the National Security Index of the American Security Council.

Don't think working people haven't noticed! Some 69% of those polled in a University of Michigan study agree that union officials do what is best for themselves—not what is best for union members.

The New Right is working hard to separate the concerns of AFL-CIO officials in Washington from the very different concerns of union leaders and members in cities and towns across the country.

That's why a group of us met with local union leaders in Youngstown, Ohio, in February, 1978. Among the New Right leaders who attended were Congressmen Phil Crane of Illinois and Mickey Edwards of Oklahoma, Howard Phillips, Paul Weyrich, John Buckley, and a few others, myself among them.

For many of us, it was an eye-opening experience. As Mickey Edwards said, "Those guys made some of us conservatives sound like moderates in comparison." The Youngstown leaders we talked to were angry about federal regulations, federal controls, and general federal involvement in the community's business.

In response, Phil Crane began putting together a legislative package emphasizing such "lunch-pail" features as a reinvestment tax credit (to encourage industries to remain in the cities) and amendments to federal environmental laws (to delay the installation of costly antipollution equipment).

The union establishment knows we're making fruitful contact with their captive membership—and they don't like it a bit. They are used to thinking of their members as the exclusive property of the unions. And so they are raging at us:

163

- The AFL-CIO has produced a $70,000 film attacking the New Right.

- William Winpisinger, president of the International Association of Machinists and Aerospace Workers, has said: "Like its spiritual predecessors in Hitler's Germany, Mussolini's Italy, and Franco's Spain, this army of the radical right has nothing but contempt for democracy and democratic institutions."

- A COPE pamphlet described me as "the godfather of the New Right," which "nourishes, grows, and funds itself on a diet of extreme antiunionism."

In other words, as Paul Weyrich has pointed out, they know they're losing. The New Right is reaching out and capturing their members' hearts. And their hysterical attacks do no good. "They are defeating themselves," Paul told the *Conservative Digest.* "Their criticism is so all-inclusive that they are causing people to look closely at what big labor leadership is all about."

Conservatives and blacks are usually assumed to be almost opposites, if not natural enemies. By the same token, liberals have succeeded in spreading the assumption that they are the blacks' best friends.

But what is the truth? Undeniably, conservatives have failed to make their case to blacks, nor were blacks particularly listening to it. But this doesn't mean there is no case to be made, that it can't be done, or that it isn't worth trying.

To begin with, liberal policies have been a disaster for blacks. Not only have they failed to solve the problems they set out to solve: they have actually made them *worse*.

Incredible? Listen to columnist Warren Brookes of the Boston *Herald-American:*

"Back in 1960, fewer than one black family in 20 was on welfare, fewer than 15% of black children were born out of wedlock to fatherless homes, and teen-age black unemployment was actually less than that for whites—about 9%.

"Today, after 20 years of massive urban and social spending programs, one black family in five is on welfare, more than 53% of all black children are born out of wedlock, and teen-age black unemployment is now pushing 40%, nearly three times that for whites. And there is widespread concern about the destruction of black family life."

Give the liberals credit. They cared. They tried to help. But their efforts backfired, and it's time for all sides to recognize it.

Take welfare, for instance. Economist Henry Hazlitt long ago pointed out that if a man makes $80 a week doing nothing, then a job that offers $100 a week in effect means that the difference between work and idleness, for him, is only $20 a week.

A system that works that way may be intended to help the needy individuals who can't find work. But in the long run, when practiced on a large scale, it undermines the moral fiber of a community.

In practice, welfare in America has served to create dependency among blacks. Worse yet, it has made many black women directly dependent on government, while making their men either economically useless or actually turning them into obstacles to acquiring welfare. Could there be a worse formula for the black family?

And yet, as Brookes goes on to say: "Despite this appalling failure of essentially liberal economic and social policies, most prominent black religious leaders, who rightly led the fight for civil rights, also support still higher levels of welfare benefits, easier standards of welfare eligibility, and a whole host of liberal social policies that would clearly contribute to a further breakdown in black family life."

Let's take a look at the effects of liberal policies on blacks.

• *Welfare.* As we've said, this is a barbed benefit. In the final analysis those who push welfare may be doing harm as surely as those who push heroin. And who is the addict's friend? The one who sells him drugs, or the one who tries to help him and cure his dependency on drugs? By accusing conservatives of "lacking compassion," liberals are in effect saying that those who hate the addiction must hate the addict.

• *Minimum wage.* This prices many blacks out of the job market. It particularly denies black teenagers the invaluable experience of entry-level jobs, where the simple disciplines required to hold down a job may be worth more than the wages in later life.

- *Affirmative action.* Not only does this policy of reverse racism breed resentment and recrimination; it sends a message to both races that blacks are incapable of making it on their own as productive, self-sufficient citizens.

- *Busing.* This policy, opposed in poll after poll by both blacks *and* whites, does nothing to improve education, creates racial tension, sends panic through whites, wastes uncounted time and money, and is *wrong.* It confirms the divisive assumption that black interests can be advanced only by hurting whites. When the two races are put at odds, it's obvious who stands to get hurt more.

- *Crime.* Some people say it's racist to talk about law and order. I would say it's racist to ignore it. Crime is heavily concentrated in black communities, victimizing men and women, old and young, and the liberals' greatest concern is still for the rights of the criminal!

- *Inflation.* Liberals used to dismiss inflation as a rich man's problem, so they advocated huge spending programs with no thought of their eventual impact on the poor—the very people who were supposed to benefit from all the spending! But if inflation is a "hidden tax," it isn't a graduated one. It hits the poor harder than other forms of taxation. Since the poor are disproportionately black, blacks are among the chief victims of liberal fiscal irresponsibility.

- *The economy.* Liberal economic policies hit the middle class first, but they hit the poor hardest. Not only inflation, but overregulation and environmentalism, though they provide jobs for white bureaucrats, create stagnation and halt the economic expansion that would spread prosperity. Instead the liberals opt for a "zero-sum society" where wealth is not created but redistributed, according to who has the most "pull." And those with "pull" aren't likely to be black.

I'd like to add a few more things about crime. Apart from insuring our country's survival, there can be no higher national priority then controlling domestic violence. The first duty of government is to protect the citizen from assault. Unless it does this, all the civil rights and civil liberties in the world aren't worth a dime.

The most basic of all rights is the right to be safe from harm. But in liberal-dominated America, safety became for all practical purposes a privilege. It turned into something that came with good real estate. Unless you could afford a "nice" neighborhood, you couldn't afford to be safe walking down the street—or even in your home.

Our goal must be to protect, not to avenge. It may come as a surprise to my friends and opponents, but I strongly oppose the death penalty. I feel that executing one or two hundred people a year is going to make almost no difference in the crime rate. I believe that a strong case can be made that Christ would oppose the killing of a human being as punishment for a crime.

I know many conservatives will disagree with me. But I feel that the most effective thing we can do to fight crime is to insure swift and certain apprehension and jailing of those who commit crime—and to give repeat offenders long jail sentences, with no early parole.

A shocking 65% of those sent to jail commit another crime and are sent back to prison. If we can keep most of the repeat offenders in jail for their full sentences, we'll probably cut the crime rate in half. It seems so simple you wonder why it's not done. A little more severity to the criminals would mean a lot more mercy to their victims.

There seems to be a law of compensation. The more needless tasks a government takes on, the worse it performs its necessary ones. Our government seems to be too busy with more important things to bother with a little matter like protecting its own law-abiding citizens.

Maybe it's only inevitable that government itself should turn criminal. I'm not just referring to the well-publicized indictments and convictions of so many of our representatives lately. I'm also thinking of the crime of inflation.

Inflation isn't just an economic problem. It's a moral problem. When our government tries to meet its debts by printing funny money, it's robbing every American. A 10% inflation rate means that a family with a $20,000 income is being robbed of $2000 a year.

Senator Jesse Helms has said it best: "Inflating the currency is tantamount to theft. It is a form of embezzlement, a 'cover operation' if there ever was one, and an immoral act."

In effect, the federal government is pouring billions of dollars of counterfeit money into the economy every year. Do you know what could happen to you if you were found guilty of counterfeiting *one* dollar?

That's why I call inflation a crime. It is a special crime against the American Dream of bettering one's lot. It strikes at the great American value of self-improvement, hurting not only the middle class but, more basically, those who would become part of the middle class.

Inflation and crime: together these two evils have wrought untold destruction on our nation's productive capabilities. They still do. But fewer and fewer criminals are being caught and punished, and not a single person has ever gone to jail for inflating the currency.

In the future the New Right will be increasing its efforts to appeal to blacks. But why should blacks listen?

• Because conservatives (not liberals) strongly disapprove of drugs and will fight to get them out of black schools and neighborhoods.

• Because conservatives (not liberals) are determined to put those who are terrorizing black neighborhoods with muggings, robbery, rape, and murder in jail for long terms.

• Because conservatives (not liberals) realize the danger of making welfare a way of life rather than just a safety net for the truly needy.

• Because conservatives (not liberals) understand that making black neighborhoods safe from crime and drugs will help bring back business and industry. And jobs.

• Because conservatives (not liberals) insist that our public schools must start teaching black children to read, write and add.

• Because conservatives (not liberals) realize the destructiveness of many well-meaning (liberal) economic and social policies.

Many so-called black "leaders" are more liberal than they are black, and just as out of touch with their supposed followers as the national union leadership. Why is it that upper-class, educated blacks like Andy Young, Carl Rowan, and Benjamin Hooks are so obsessed with South Africa and Zimbabwe? Where are the black leaders who are talking about the real problems of blacks in America?

Someday there will emerge a true American black leader. He will point out that today's black emperors have no clothes on.

He will demand that schools really teach black children the basics and that disruptive children be expelled. He will demand that black neighborhoods be made safe from murder, robbery, rape, and drugs.

This black leader will point out how most black leaders of the past 30 years have led blacks down a path of slavery, deceit, and poverty. It's white and black liberals who are the modern day Simon Legrees. It's the liberals with their Dark Age ideas who would put blacks in bondage to the master called big government.

This new black leader may already be among us. The name may be Parker, or Wilson, or Thomas, or McKee, or Williams.

J.A. Parker, a black who is president of the Lincoln Institute and editor of *The Lincoln Review*, has the right idea: "The billions of dollars of government money are no longer there. The well is almost dry at the federal level. The answer lies in more productivity, more growth, and more jobs."

Margaret Bush Wilson, chairman of the NAACP, agrees. She has firmly stated her opposition to the liberals' no-growth philosophy of energy. Of Jimmy Carter's 1977 less-energy plan, Mrs. Wilson observed that it had been drawn up by people "who would subscribe to a limits-of-growth philosophy" which would freeze people to whatever rung of the economic ladder they happen to be on. That's okay if you're a highly educated 23-year-old making $50,000 a year as a presidential advisor. It's utter disaster if you're unskilled, out of work, and living in a ghetto."

Lawyer Clarence Thomas, an aide to Sen. John Danforth (R—Mo.) and a black who made it through Yale without benefit of quotas, says: "I'm tired of blacks

169

being thought of only as poor people, people on welfare, people who are unemployed. That's the only way Jesse Jackson and the other black leaders talk about black people. To them, we're all a monolith. Well, they are not talking for the 80 to 90% of black people in this country who have never been on welfare or in jail."

Another black lawyer, Clarence McKee, agrees: "Although we must never forget our obligations to the poor and those who have been victims of various inequities because of race and birth, we must also not forget those of the black middle class—people who have worked hard, depite obstacles, to become participating and self-sufficient members of our society. It is from this group that the black youth of our country find role models to use as examples of success in their lives."

Economist Walter E. Williams of Temple University has been critical of the established black leadership for many years. Their major error, he says, was "making government largess a way of life for a large segment of the black population." He blames this on "the wedding-of-convenience between black politicians, white union officials, and the Democratic Party.

"It's convenient to everyone—except the black voters, who are consistent losers in this arrangement."

Professor Williams offers this conclusion: "The lesson to be learned from this unfortunate trend is that blacks are in the unenviable position where Democrats can get their votes without earning them, and Republicans won't even try, because they are confident they won't get them. Worst of all, black political leaders have come to feel they have a monopoly on the black vote, and they can take it for granted—no matter how misguided this blind loyalty may be."

All these blacks have learned what we in the New Right have come to realize: that dependency, whether on government or on a single political party, is a short route to helplessness.

Unlike liberals, these blacks have nothing against the American middle class. They would just like to see more blacks in it!

XV

Can Reagan Keep His Base?

In the last chapter I pointed out the liberals' mistake of taking two groups—blue-collar workers and blacks—for granted. And earlier I mentioned Jimmy Carter's fatal mistake of doing the same thing with born-again Christians.

I sense a danger that President Reagan may be making a similar mistake by underestimating the importance of his conservative supporters.

I'm not talking about sharing the spoils. I'm not even talking about gratitude to old friends. I'm talking about something more hard-headed and practical—something that will affect the future course of the nation.

Ronald Reagan doesn't need to water down his conservative principles now. His conservative principles got him elected. Time and again, as his whole career shows, it was when he was truest to those principles that he attracted previously indifferent voters.

Ronald Reagan, of all people, doesn't need to take lessons in how to succeed in politics from the same people—liberals and "moderate" Republicans—who have brought both parties and the country so close to ruin. They are the same people he has just routed.

It's easy to see why those people are so eager to give him advice. It's harder to see why he should even consider taking it. He should look to his own, to the conservatives who have formed the vital core of his support. Not only because he owes it to them, but—more importantly—because the principles he shares with them have *already* broadened his base to a majority of the American electorate.

Broadening your base and watering down your principles are two different things. In fact they are opposites.

Consider the liberal churches. Many liberal Christians always think they can make Christianity more attractive by watering it down. But they're wrong. All they succeed in doing is making Christianity more "acceptable" to people who aren't about to become Christians anyway. Only the conservative churches manage to satisfy people who hunger for truth and guidance. Result: liberal denominations lose members, while conservative churches continue to attract, grow, and make a difference.

We don't want to sound like the rooster who thought his crowing caused the sun to rise. Ronald Reagan might have won without us on November 4. He is an extremely attractive personality and a great campaigner, and 1980 was a challenger's year.

Yes, he might have won on November 4 no matter who supported him. But how did he happen to be on the ballot? Without strong conservative grass-roots organization, Ronald Reagan would never have gotten as far as he did.

Since President Reagan was elected, we've seen traditional Republicans and some of the media say President Reagan is not indebted to the conservatives for his election.

This, of course, is incorrect. The people who make these self serving statements have an interest in making the President and the public think it was the traditional political establishment that is most responsible for Reagan's victory.

However, the Republican establishment has opposed President Reagan from the start of his political career in 1965 until the spring of 1980 when he locked up the Republican nomination.

172

These moderate and liberal Republicans remind me of the old saying that defeat is an orphan and victory has many fathers.

It is certainly true President Reagan was elected because he received the votes of Democrats as well as Republicans, of conservatives and moderates. Voters in every section of America supported him.

But let me point out that President Reagan did not go directly from Hollywood to the White House.

There were many political battles along the way. It started with the Republican primary for governor of California in 1966 against a moderate, former San Francisco mayor George Christopher, and a liberal candidate.

The hardcore conservative activists provided the base of Reagan's support—they contributed money, they manned the phones, they walked the precincts, and they beat the moderate and liberal candidates.

For the 8 years while he was governor, it was conservative magazines like *National Review* and *Human Events* along with numerous conservative columnists like Bill Rusher, Morrie Ryskind, John Chamberlain, Phyllis Schlafly, John Lofton, Stan Evans, Dean Manion and Bill Buckley that helped make Reagan a popular national figure.

Reagan was the main speaker at hundreds of rallies and meetings sponsored by conservative organizations like the A.C.U., Y.A.F. and the New York Conservative Party. These functions helped Reagan build his political army that would later do battle nationally with the moderates and the liberals.

And during the period from 1965 to 1976 while the conservative movement was united in the project of building Ronald Reagan into the most popular conservative in America, he was continually opposed by the moderates and liberals.

Despite his meteoric rise and well-deserved success, he had some shaky moments.

When Reagan announced for President in 1975, he had next to no support other than from the grass-root supporters of the conservative movement and their young leaders. In the U.S. Senate, only Paul Laxalt and Jesse Helms supported Reagan.

Even establishment conservatives like Barry Goldwater, John Tower and Jake Garn opposed Reagan and supported Jerry Ford.

In 1976, Reagan didn't have political bigwigs on his team. It was 180,000 conservatives who financed Reagan's campaign. Millions more volunteered to work and voted for Reagan against the moderate liberal Jerry Ford.

In February 1976, Ford narrowly beat Reagan in the New Hampshire primary. Ten days later Ford soundly defeated Reagan in the Florida primary.

Reagan seemed to be facing defeat for the first and last time of his political career. Many national Republican leaders publicly suggested that now was the time for Reagan to hang up his spurs, withdraw from the presidential race and support Jerry Ford.

Reagan had a lot to be proud of and apparently little to look forward to. An honorable retirement seemed like the natural next step.

But in the dark hours for Reagan, two of America's greatest and most important conservatives, Senator Jesse Helms and Tom Ellis came to his rescue and saved him from having to retire from politics. His conservative friends wouldn't let him quit.

First, they very strongly urged Reagan to come out and attack Ford for wanting to give away the Panama Canal, keeping Henry Kissinger as Secretary of State and engaging in detente with the Soviets.

Reagan took their advice and come out slugging against Ford.

Helms had been elected, eighteen months earlier, as the first Republican Senator from North Carolina since Reconstruction. Tom Ellis as Helms' friend and campaign manager had organized conservatives in North Carolina into a sophisticated political operation.

Helms and Ellis now went back to these thousands of hardcore conservatives and asked them to work to help Ronald Reagan beat Jerry Ford in the North Carolina primary.

When the conservatives woke up on the morning after the primary to hear that Reagan had beaten Ford by 52% to 48%, it electrified conservatives nationally. Ronald Reagan's win in North Carolina propelled him to another major primary victory in Texas. New life was breathed into the Reagan campaign. It became a close fight again. It was one of the most exciting challenges to a sitting President the GOP had ever seen. And it made him the front runner for the 1980 Republican nomination.

And, again, throughout 1979 and 1980 when Reagan was running in Republican primaries, it was the hardcore conservative movement led by *Human Events*, Paul Laxalt, Jesse Helms, Orrin Hatch, Mickey Edwards, Bob Dornan, Bob Heckman, Terry Dolan and NCPAC, YAF, ACU, Tom Ellis and the Congressional Club, and many other conservatives who provided over 90% of this support.

In fact, Reagan was at best the fourth choice of Big Business, Establishment Republicans. Their first, second and third choices were Connally, Bush and Baker.

And, of course, no reasonable scenario for Reagan's landslide victory in 1980 could be constructed without the overwhelming support he received from this nation's evangelical Christian conservatives. Especially when you consider the support this group gave to Jimmy Carter in 1976.

Perhaps no other segment of the American population is more disturbed about what's happening to our country than these fundamentally conservative Christians.

I've already talked about the role of Jerry Falwell's "Moral Majority" and their work in registering millions of Christian voters, and getting them to the polls and getting them to work and vote for Ronald Reagan.

I've also mentioned the major role played by people like Ed McAteer, who, in 1979 organized the Religious Roundtable. From July to October of 1980, Ed organized public affairs briefings from Florida to California attended by 40,000 conservative and religious leaders including over 20,000 ministers.

At a single religious roundtable public affairs briefing in Dallas, Ronald Reagan spoke to 18,000 religious leaders. This superbly organized event which drew major media attention was put together by the Rev. James Robison, one of the key leaders in the New Christian Right.

The payoff of this intense pre-election effort by Falwell, McAteer, Robison, and others was, in my opinion, the landslide proportions of Ronald Reagan's win in November.

Every conservative has been deeply encouraged by President Reagan's early pronouncements. In his inaugural message and his first press conference he has sounded themes dear to our hearts on the primacy of religion, the importance of the productive sector, and the continuing Soviet threat. It's been a long time since we heard such stirring rhetoric coming from our nation's leadership—rhetoric that expresses the vital truths we had strayed from.

And he has given us more than rhetoric. He has appointed some top-notch people. I'm thinking of David Stockman of the OMB, UN representative Jeane Kirkpatrick, Secretary of Labor Ray Donovan, and Interior Secretary James Watt.

And yet, today, there is not one outspoken born again Christian in the Reagan Cabinet. There are only a few conservative activists. There is no one representing blue collar Democrats, no conservative black, and no one representing Phyllis Schlafly and the conservative women's movement.

When you think of the support candidate Ronald Reagan has had from the conservative movement since 1964—support that has remained absolutely unwavering even in the face of crushing electoral defeats and the opposition of almost every major GOP official—you have to ask, why does it seem we're being ignored and overlooked by President Reagan.

Most every conservative I've talked to since President Reagan started to put together his White House team has told me they are disappointed.

In fact, even many members of the national media have asked me what's happening—they ask why is Reagan choosing moderates and mostly ignoring conservatives?

The New Right has never been interested in political power for its own sake. That is what makes us different from the Republican establishment, who have no clear ideals to guide them in exercising the power they covet so much (on the rare occasions when they achieve it).

When I'm asked why Reagan isn't appointing conservatives, I explain that I am disappointed that the majority of policy making positions in the Reagan Administration have gone to the moderates and liberals. However, I am not going to spend any significant time thinking about it.

I am urging all conservatives to not dwell on the past but to spend the next 3 years (1981 through 1983) increasing the size and strength of the conservative movement. Let's develop a three year plan to grow by 4 to 5 times over our present strength.

The New Right has come from very little in 1975 to represent a significant force in American politics in 1981.

With the momentum we have going for us and with smart, hard work, we will by 1984 have attained the strength that the liberals had in the 1950s and 1960s.

Shakespeare wrote, "There is a tide in the affairs of men which taken at the flood leads on to fortune."

Conservatives have been presented with such an opportunity. It is now our challenge and our duty to our fellow man to mount the wave and ride it to victory and freedom for all of mankind.

Let's all put our shoulder to the wheel and redouble our efforts. Most conservative organizations should be able to increase the size of their organizations four hundred to five hundred percent by January 1984.

The Viguerie Company's clients have on computer the names and addresses of 4,500,000 people who have said in the past few years they are conservative on one or more issues.

We at The Viguerie Company have developed a plan to double that to 9,000,000 by 1984.

We now have 40 clients. We will double our creative staff in 1981 (from 15 to 30) and double the number of our clients by 1982.

I hope to increase the number of subscribers to *Conservative Digest* from 60,000 to 200,000 and to start six new conservative publications by 1982.

I also expect to start a book club for conservatives in 1981.

In other words, I plan to follow my own advice to work to greatly increase the strength of the conservative movement.

I hope all conservatives will do the same so that by 1984 the eastern big business moderate and liberal Democrats and Republicans will no longer be the major force in American politics.

My purpose in this chapter is simply to point out the deep and permanent sources of Ronald Reagan's support.

He has always risen on the tide of conservatism. Even where he did best on November 4, 1980, he got an extra boost from the existence of a powerful conservative organization beneath him. And in some states he actually ran behind other conservatives!

Without the New Right, Candidate Ronald Reagan would have pulled something less than 50% of the total popular vote. His election would have appeared less as a mandate for himself than as a rejection of Jimmy Carter. And pollster Lou Harris calculates that Reagan owed *two thirds* of his victory margin to white evangelical Christians, the Moral Majority and associated groups who switched from Carter in 1976.

But that's only part of the story.

Without the New Right, President Reagan would have faced a Congress still dominated by liberal Democrats in both Houses. His role today would have been one of opposition, vetoing liberal Democratic initiatives, rather than one of real leadership, able to set the agenda and shape the future.

He would have had to put up with many of the same crew Richard Nixon faced: George McGovern, Frank Church, Dick Clark, Tom McIntyre, Birch Bayh, Gaylord Nelson, Warren Magnuson—some or all of these would have remained in the Senate as part of the Democratic majority.

But with the help of the New Right, Ronald Reagan sits today in the White House with a Republican Senate, a much more conservative House of Representatives, and an American public who has been sold on conservative ideas.

And by being true to the solid core of his support, President Reagan can keep his new American majority based on a strong and lasting foundation.

XVI

We're Ready to Lead!

We're just beginning. And the future is wide open.

As the Bible says, there is a time for everything under heaven—a time to be born, and a time to die; a time to break down, and a time to build up; a time to keep silent, and a time to speak; a time of war, and a time of peace.

I think it is a time to lead.

We've already made such tremendous gains that some people assume we must have already fulfilled our basic potential. Frankly, I might have thought so too—except for one thing.

We've surpassed our early goals by so much that I've learned to quit expecting to run up against a final limit.

It isn't just the liberals who have been shocked by our successes. Even some of our conservative allies have been stunned. They're glad, of course, but they can't quite believe it's really happening.

Perhaps if I had been in the foxholes for 30 years as a lot of conservatives have, if I had been shot at and shelled and torn apart and suffered as many defeats as they've suffered, I might have a defeatist attitude too.

But life teaches you to be ready for anything—even success.

And we're ready. We of the New Right believe that we will prevail.

Several years ago, Phyllis Schlafly asked Dr. Fred Schwarz what did he think was the Communists' greatest asset, and before he could reply Phyllis answered her own question. She said she felt the Communists' greatest asset was their total conviction that they will win.

There isn't a Communist leader in the world worth his salt who doesn't feel that Communism is the wave of the future.

That's what conservatives have going for them now. New Right conservatives believe that we will govern America. And we believe that freedom is the wave of the future.

A lot of older conservatives did not see themselves as winning and governing America. They saw themselves as sometimes influencing those who governed, but they did not see themselves as governing.

When Martin Luther nailed his 95 theses to the church door, he didn't know he was launching the biggest revolution in the history of Europe. Like everyone else in his time, he assumed that there would always be one all-inclusive Church.

But within a few years the entire face of the continent was changed. I believe that something similar, on a smaller scale, is now happening in America.

Like Luther, American conservatives didn't set out to make radical changes—just to restore some basic principles. But we've found that the ancient truths require new actions.

Our new reality has been achieved—though only partially so far—in the New Right, a network nearly as vast and complex as all the new Reformed churches that sprang up in Europe in Luther's time. If the Reformation could occur so swiftly in the age of the printing press and the horse-drawn carriage, think of how fast America can change in the age of television, computers, and jet planes!

Think of the established media as being like the medieval Church, and you begin to grasp why people are alarmed by the New Right. People are used to getting their messages from certain familiar sources: the major networks, the newspapers and wire services, the schools and universities, the pollsters and experts.

CBS may be a private organization, but there is something so official-seeming about Walter Cronkite.

I don't just mean that the established media are liberal in their orientation. That's only part of it, and maybe not even the most important part.

It's something different. People are used to being guided by these media not only in what to think, but in what to think *about*. They expect the media not to dictate opinion (which most people in the media conscientiously try to avoid doing) but to announce the agenda.

The pollsters are willing to let you give your own answers, but you're probably accustomed to letting them choose the questions.

The result of this is that what we call "public opinion" is highly artificial. It may tell you in a general way what most people feel about the items on the liberal agenda. It doesn't answer the deeper question of how they feel about the agenda itself.

They may care very little about things the liberals feel strongly about, like the Equal Rights Amendment. They may hide their real feelings and give the answers they think the pollsters expect, because they think it's "unenlightened," or "bad taste," or may be seen as a sign of a "lack of compassion" to give non-liberal answers. They may not even realize there *are* non-liberal answers. So the responses people give to the polls are often formalistic and misleading.

For all these reasons, polls can be used to make it appear there is a national mandate for liberal policies, when in fact there just isn't. Don't think it doesn't happen!

Columnist Joseph Sobran has defined public opinion as "what everyone thinks everyone else thinks." That's an apt way of describing the barrier the New Right has had to break down.

Public opinion of this kind has another serious defect. It doesn't include all the things people may think and talk and care about when they're among themselves, without any liberal supervision around—the things the liberals would often prefer not to hear about anyway, and even discourage people from mentioning in public.

As the years have passed and the media have grown in influence, something else has grown too: a widening gap between "public opinion" and the real concerns of Americans.

It isn't just a gap. It's become a real tension, as the liberal program has been imposed often in direct opposition to what the American people would really prefer.

As I said at the beginning of this book, the media have given very little attention to subjects like school prayer and Communist aggression. A study by Dr. Ernest Lefever of Georgetown University found that the CBS Evening News had devoted only *one minute* to the Soviet arms buildup over a *two-year period!* And naturally enough, TV has given very little coverage to one of its own "pocketbook issues": immorality on TV.

Is it any wonder the New Right has sought to break free of the established mass communications system with its own independent channels of communication?

And is it any wonder we make them and the people who have innocently relied on them a little uneasy?

Our power is the ignored and untapped power of millions of ordinary Americans who want to hear another side and make some contribution of their own. We're trying to answer a profound need in American life. The results speak for themselves.

The American people believe in the separation of church and state. They don't believe in the segregation of traditional morality and public life.

Many who were alarmed by us at first are discovering that while we may be a little unorthodox, they basically agree with us. This has even been known to happen to liberals! Some of them too have come to feel that while tolerance is a fine thing, enough is enough.

One of the few conservatives who rejected the attitude that the nation was somehow doomed to eternal liberalism was the late Professor Willmoore Kendall. He long ago perceived that liberalism was riding for a fall, and that it was placing intolerable strains on the patience of the American people and on their deepest traditions.

Kendall predicted that when all the pockets of resistance to the liberal program had had enough, they would get in touch with each other and fight back. And in the showdown, he added, liberalism would lose.

That's exactly what is happening today.

Conservatism isn't the special philosophy of a fringe group. It's the American mainstream. That's why we *know* we're going to win.

Today, as Jeffrey Hart has observed, it's the liberal *New York Times*, not the conservative *National Review*, that seems like the "fringe" publication.

The liberals have done a good job of impersonating a mainstream, and they have succeeded in winning an extension for their unnatural dominance in public life.

They should have lost in 1974, and in 1976. But each time they succeeded in improvising, with issues like Watergate and with a Southern presidential candidate who was able to patch together the old Democratic coalition for a last hurrah, while the Republican Party failed to provide conservative leadership.

But deep down, they knew it wasn't solid. Today, some of the hard-core liberals know their time is up, and many of their own faithful are defecting. They can't pretend we aren't here, as they did for so many years. At the moment they are pretending we pose a threat to the Constitution they have so badly abused, but this is only a desperate, rear-guard action to rally their remaining troops.

It won't last. In a few months—a few years, at most— they will have to concede defeat and step aside. The 1980 elections were a big victory for conservatives. We won a battle, not the war.

But our final triumph won't happen automatically. All the conditions are favorable. But we still have to *make* it happen, just as much as when we set out, many years ago, to fight our first lonely battles.

There won't be a formal surrender. Pockets of liberal resistance will remain for a long time—after all, they've ruled the roost for at least half a century. The framers of our constitutional system created a wonderfully durable and complex political order, one that has withstood many determined assaults, and no single party—not even conservatives—can or should take it over all at once.

And let's not forget the many positive contributions of liberals themselves. For all their excesses, they have helped America to see and correct blind spots with respect to blacks, women, prisoners, and various other victims of injustice. We want liberals out of power. We don't want them out of the country.

Meanwhile, there is work to be done.

Conservatives have a lot of good ideas to make America a better place to live and work in. But I can't say it enough: the basic ingredient now is *leadership*. That's what the New Right has to offer. But we can't get too much of it. There has never been a leadership surplus.

I feel that most of the problems the cause of freedom faces in America and in the world today arise from a lack of leadership. Most of them could be corrected if we had a few more good leaders.

If you think about it, this country is here today because of a few dozen people. If there had been no Washington, no Franklin, no Jefferson, no Adams, plus 20 others some 200 years ago we might still be a colony of Great Britain.

Starting in the early 1930s, we did not graduate from the universities or colleges future conservative leaders.

For some reason, we conservatives skipped an entire generation of leaders.

As a result, in the 1950s, 1960s and 1970s the Left had their Humphreys, Stevensons, Kennedys, Rockefellers, Javits, Mondales and Reuthers.

But the right had very few leaders during these three decades.

We did have a fair number of people who were well-known and articulate, good writers, good debaters, who had charisma.

And most people would think that they were leaders. But only in the last few years did I come to understand that most were spokesmen. They were not leaders.

A leader will make things happen, he will start a new organization or a new magazine. He will call meetings, suggest assignments, then call a follow-up meeting to review the progress.

A leader realizes that winners have plans and losers have excuses.

There is a big difference between a spokesman and a leader. It's not that a spokesman is not important; it's just that you need both spokesmen *and* leaders. But for many years conservatives had spokesmen but very few leaders.

184

But starting in the 1950s and early 1960s we started to produce from our universities and colleges those who have gone on to provide the critically needed conservative leadership.

First came Bill Buckley, Bill Rusher, Stan Evans, and Phyllis Schlafly, then, in rapid succession, Howard Phillips, Carol and Bob Bauman, Jesse Helms, Jerry Falwell, Jameson Campaigne, Orrin Hatch, Mickey Edwards, Paul Weyrich, James Robison, Morton Blackwell, Terry Dolan and many, many others.

While the conservative leadership gap is being filled, the liberals are rapidly losing their leadership. And it will be at least ten years before the kids who were in the streets marching against the war in Vietnam will be old enough to provide leadership for the Left.

It appears to me that the 1980s will see the liberals suffering from a serious leadership gap.

This provides an enormous opportunity for the conservatives to take charge of the major institutions in America while the left is not playing with a full team.

However, we need lots more leaders—and at all levels, not just in Washington.

I'd like *you*, personally, to give some serious thought to becoming a leader. You might think about becoming a candidate for the school board, city council, state legislature or Congress. Or perhaps you might seek a position in your local Democratic or Republican organization.

Don't sell yourself short by thinking you don't have the talent or ability or background to run for or hold public office.

Very few people who hold public office are genuine giants. They are people for the most part like you and me —engineers, housewives, doctors, concerned parents, salesmen.

Don't make the mistake of waiting for a committee of the leading citizens of your community to plead with you to run for Congress, or mayor, or city council, or the board of education.

Occasionally, it does work that way. But if Jimmy Carter had waited for a committee to plead with him, he'd still be waiting in Plains, Georgia.

Orrin Hatch, a Salt Lake City attorney with no political experience, decided to make his plunge in 1976. He now represents Utah in the U.S. Senate.

Gordon Humphrey, an Allegheny Airlines co-pilot who had never run for public office, decided to provide some leadership in 1978. Gordon did not have the support of any big name New Hampshire political leaders, only his own friends, his associates from The New Hampshire Conservative Caucus and a few New Right national leaders. He now represents New Hampshire in the U.S. Senate.

There are many more Orrin Hatches and Gordon Humphreys in America—conservatives who can and must make a contribution now to their country.

For the past 50 years, conservatives have stressed almost exclusively economic and foreign policy. The New Right shares the same basic beliefs of other conservatives in economics and foreign policy matters, but we feel that conservatives cannot become the dominant political force in America until we stress the issues of concern to ethnic and blue collar Americans, born-again Christians, pro-life Catholics and Jews.

Some of these issues are busing, quotas, crime, abortion, pornography, education and traditional Biblical moral values.

However, there are certain qualities that the New Right has that previous conservatives didn't have.

As a general rule, New Right conservatives are young. They are aggressive, sharp, tough, work long hours, meet often, develop strategy, plans and tactics, cooperate with Democrats, Independents and Republicans, use and understand new technology. Their day is filled with activities designed to replace liberals with conservatives in all major American institutions.

They are conservatives who are tired of losing and are personally committed to bringing freedom to America and the world in the near future. And they have a firm conviction that they will succeed.

What keeps conservatives like Jesse Helms, that dedicated, tireless "conscience of the Senate," going? He has the following motto on a plaque in his Senate office, and I've adopted it as a guide for my life:

"God does not require me to succeed, but He does require me to try."

Frankly, I think He requires all of us to try.

As I said at the very beginning of this book, the left is old and tired. We in the New Right are young and vigorous.

Many of the liberals' leaders like Adlai Stevenson, Nelson Rockefeller, Hubert Humphrey, Robert and Jack Kennedy are gone. Our leaders are coming into their own.

The liberals had a lot of victories over the last 50 years. But they've grown soft and sluggish. They have lost confidence in themselves and in their ideas.

We're lean, determined and hungry—to gain victories for conservatism and to renew our great country.

Yes, the tide is turning. It is turning our way—freedom's way.

EPILOGUE:
DEAR MR. PRESIDENT

If I had the opportunity to spend a few minutes with President Reagan, I would offer him the following advice:

Mr. President, I'd like to call to your attention some danger signals I see on the horizon.

You were a good governor in California. That's not just a compliment from me. Most objective political observers agree.

But unfortunately, your achievements didn't last. After you completed your eight years in office, the liberals took over the state's power structures—the Governor's office, most other statewide elected offices, and both houses of the legislature.

They've held them ever since.

The State of California enjoyed a Reagan Administration. But today it lacks elected leaders devoted to continuing the type of government you gave California.

To be blunt, Mr. President, you apparently gave little thought to building a Conservative/Republican power base in California to help insure that those who shared your views would govern long after you left office.

And I see alarming signs that this pattern is about to be repeated in your presidency.

The average age of your cabinet officers is 51 years old. I feel you should appoint very few in their fifties. And the average age of your sub-cabinet appointees should be under 45. You need to be appointing hundreds and even thousands of people in their 30s and 40s who are bright, have potential and are politically ambitious. You must build a new generation of conservatives who will go back to the their home states to run for Congress, governor and the state legislature. We are counting on your administration to provide thousands of conservatives with the credentials which will help advance their political or professional career.

Also, consideration needs to be given to appointing conservatives from areas where conservatives are weak and where we need an infusion of young leadership.

While we can always use more young conservative leaders in Utah, North Carolina, South Carolina, and Idaho, it is much more important in the effort to strengthen the conservatives nationally to seek out conservatives in our weaker states. (For example, we need more conservative leaders in Vermont, Oregon, Maine, Delaware, Massachusetts, Connecticut, and Rhode Island.)

As you know, between 1965 and the spring of 1980 about the only people to support you were the hardcore conservatives in America. The rest thought you couldn't win or just plain didn't want you to.

But today, in the early stages of your Presidency, the message is coming through loud and clear that few staunch Reaganites need apply for important policy-making positions.

I understand the need to reach out and to reconcile. That's a sound and generous impulse.

But you can't do these things meaningfully unless you first hold on to your original base. The first law of politics is that you have to reward your supporters. If you appoint only people who share half of your views—or even less—you'll be judged as just another shifty politician. Most Americans, regardless of persuasion, have had enough of that kind. They've decided you are different.

And how can you put your principles into effect if most key policy-making positions in your Administration are held by non-conservatives?

I can't overstress the need to include large numbers of the young people who have worked their hearts out for you these last five years. If you fail to do that, many of them will be soured on politics, and a whole generation of potential conservative leaders will be damaged.

America needs a rebirth of religious commitment. I urge you to use your great skills as a communicator and regularly ask people to seek the solution to our personal and national problems in God.

Consider setting aside one or more days a year devoted to prayer, fasting, and mediation in which we thank God for our blessings, our opportunities, our freedoms, our great country and ask for deliverance from our enemies.

Encourage people to visit the sick, prisoners, the dying, feed the hungry and help the poor.

Your personal example, along with Mrs. Reagan's, can help lead America to a rebirth of greatness.

I applaud your practice of working only 40-50 hours a week when you were Governor and I hope you continue that practice as President. But just as you need balance in your life, those who are entrusted with important responsibilities in your administration also need balance in their life. Their performance will suffer if their personal life and family life is not healthy.

So remember if 40-50 hours per week works for you, it would probably be good for your aides.

Most of the people you've appointed, while they may be nice and decent people, will not be able to help put together future election victories.

The traditional moderate/liberal wing of the G.O.P. has been trying to figure out since 1930 how to win elections. And of course they have failed miserably. It seems the only way Republicans can capture the presidency is with a candidate perceived to be a conservative.

You received the Republican nomination for President and a big election victory November 4th along with a much more conservative House and Senate because thousands of prominent religious leaders, pro-gun leaders, pro-life leaders, and pro-family leaders went to their supporters and passed the word loud and clear to vote for you.

Now in the first three months since you were elected President leaders of the Christian Right are not even able to have a single meeting with you.

Remember, you personally assured these ministers during the 1980 election in a meeting in your hotel room in Washington, D.C. that you would give the Christian Right representation in your administration appropriate to their numbers nationally.

There will be many times during the next few years when you and the Republican Party will want their help.

You apparently have not instructed your top appointees to make sure that your administration is staffed only with people who share your views and values. If you had done this, you would not have selected Terrel Bell to head the education department. Bell supports busing and strongly supported the establishment of the education department.

Unfortunately, Terrel Bell is not an isolated example. You have filled your administration with many people who have fought and opposed conservatives for many years.

Naturally, we can't help wondering why there is such a gap between the way you've talked for sixteen years and some of the things you've done since your election.

The New Right, I can assure you, wants to be your friend and strong supporter. But we won't be political Uncle Toms. We learned our lesson in the Nixon-Ford years.

We share a common goal with you. We want you to be the best President the U.S. has had in the 20th century. And I firmly believe you can be—simply by being the same man the American people have known, admired, and elected.

Sincerely,

Richard A. Viguerie

Appendix A

Conservative Publications and Organizations

For those of you who want to get more involved in the conservative movement, I have put together the following list of three major publications and seven major organizations and PACs.

Conservative Digest (monthly)
7777 Leesburg Pike
Falls Church, VA 22043
Annual subscription: $15

Human Events (weekly)
422 First Street, S.E.
Washington, D.C. 20003
Annual subscription: $25

National Review (26 issues yearly)
150 East 35th Street
New York, N.Y. 10016
Annual subscription: $24

American Conservative Union
Suite 400
316 Pennsylvania Avenue, S.E.
Washington, D.C. 20003

Committee for the Survival of a Free Congress
721 Second Street, N.E.
Washington, D.C. 20002

Conservative Victory Fund
422 First Street, S.E.
Washington, D.C. 20003

National Conservative Political Action
   Committee
Suite 513
1500 Wilson Boulevard
Arlington, VA 22209

The Conservative Caucus
422 Maple Avenue, East
Vienna, VA 22180

The Congressional Club
Suite 300
3825 Barrett Drive
Raleigh, N.C. 27609

Fund For The Conservative Majority
1022 Wilson Boulevard
Arlington, VA 22209

Appendix B

National Day of Prayer and Fasting Petition to Elected Public Officials

We the undersigned do respectfully petition you, our elected leaders, to help bring America back to God by setting aside the Sunday before each Thanksgiving as a National Day of Fasting and Prayer.

Just as we celebrate the bounty of God's blessing on Thanksgiving Day with the traditional family meal, we will set aside the Sunday before Thanksgiving as a day of fast and prayer to bring us closer to God.

We will fast and pray as Jesus and Moses did, so that we will be strengthened to meet the many serious challenges facing our nation.

We will humbly pray that God lead our nation through the many dangers that lie ahead and to restore His blessing on the American people.

Many of our personal and national problems have developed because we have forgotten to thank God for our blessings, our opportunities, our freedoms and our great country.

_____

Name

_____

Address

_____

City, state & zip

_____

Name

_____

Address

_____

City, state & zip

Send copies of this petition to public officials such as mayors, city councilmen, governors, Congressmen.

_____
Name

_____
Address

_____
City, state & zip

_____
Name

_____
Address

_____
City, state & zip

_____
Name

_____
Address

_____
City, state & zip

_____
Name

_____
Address

_____
City, state & zip

_____
Name

_____
Address

_____
City, state & zip

_____
Name

_____
Address

_____
City, state & zip

Send copies of this petition to public officials such as mayors, city councilmen, governors, Congressmen.

Index